The Great PHYSICIAN

Luke: The Healing Stories

Revised and Expanded

LINDSEY P. PHERIGO

Abingdon Press

Nashville

THE GREAT PHYSICIAN:
Luke—The Healing Stories

Revised Edition

Copyright © 1983, 1991 by Lindsey P. Pherigo

Formerly published as *The Great Physician The Healing Stories in Luke and their Meaning for Today* by The Education and Cultivation Division, for the Women's Division, General Board of Global Ministries, The United Methodist Church.

All rights reserved.

Library of Congress Cataloging-in-Publication Data

Pherigo, Lindsey P.
    The great physician: Luke, the healing stories / Lindsey P. Pherigo.
        p.   cm. — (Abingdon lay Bible studies)
    Includes bibliographical references.
    ISBN 0-687-15788-9
    1. Jesus Christ—Miracles. 2. Bible, N.T. Luke—Criticism, interpretation, etc. 3. Spiritual healing.   I. Title.   II. Series.
BT366.P52   1991
226.7'06—dc20   90-21917
                                                        CIP

ISBN 0-687-15788-9

Scripture quotations, except where specifically noted, are from the Revised Standard Version of the Bible, copyright © 1946, 1952, © 1971 by the Division of Christian Education, National Council of Churches of christ in the U.S.A. Used by permission.

Manufactured in the United States of America

ACKNOWLEDGMENTS

My greatest debts are to my two editors: I gladly credit them for whatever readability this final product possesses. My official editor, Nancy A. Carter, has been patient beyond all expectations with the delays caused by my unexpected open-heart surgery just at the time the first draft was scheduled for completion. In addition to her patience, she has made several skillful arrangements of materials that greatly clarified what I wanted to say. My unofficial editor, Rebecca Hoge, has worked over the entire manuscript with me, in all of its drafts, exposing mannerisms I was unaware of, systematically changing passive verb forms to active, flagging unnecessary prejudices and personal opinions that violated my aim to be non-judgmental and helping me break the material into meaningful units.

I owe substantial debts to several others. Susan Halverstadt read the entire manuscript from the perspective of her expertise in health matters, helped with discussion options, and contributed many helpful suggestions. Two women were of special help from a religious and educational perspective. Frances Manson, associate pastor at Indian Heights United Methodist Church in Overland Park, Kansas, raised my consciousness level on several matters of common prejudice. Carole Mehl, Director of Christian Education at Central United Methodist Church in Kansas City, Missouri, brought some of the more abstract material down to earth, and at the same time raised some deeper questions than I could handle. Richard Athey, psychological counsellor at The Village Church in Prairie Village, Kansas, saved me some embarrassment by correcting several slips. Physician Max Miller, also of Village Church, provided me with valuable data about "spontaneous remissions" as understood in the medical world. Criticisms and suggestions from individual members of the Committees on Program and Spiritual and Theological Concerns of the Women's Division, which read each draft, have made the work stronger in every way.

Many others have given me the encouragement and support I needed to get myself deeply involved in an aspect of the Gospel of Luke that I had not previously explored in depth. Among these my colleague at Village Church, Rena Yocom, Minister of Adult Education, stands out clearly. More in the background are many adults in my classes at Village Church who were willing to hear and react to the ideas I had at the beginning of this research: their names are legion.

A special note of appreciation is due my long-suffering wife, Viola. This project has taken many, many hours out of the time we ordinarily spend together. Her complaints are justified, and yet she shares in my sense of accomplishment and has co-operated at every stage with generous understanding and full support.

For this revision, I have profited greatly by the expertise of Karen Hall, my typist. She has given me many helpful suggestions for clarifying the text of the three new chapters.

Chapter Eleven is a revision of a paper I prepared for the University of Kansas Medical School's annual Symposia on Religion and Health. Chapters Twelve and Thirteen are revisions and adaptations of my Wertsch Lectures of 1985 at Saint Paul School of Theology. I am grateful to both schools for the opportunity to develop these topics.

September 15, 1990
Kansas City, Missouri

CONTENTS

FOREWORD

All of the early Christian traditions about Jesus in his earthly life remember him as one vitally concerned about the total well-being of individuals. The Gospels stress his reputation as a healer. Luke's Gospel gives special attention to the concern of Jesus for total health. This book is a special study of the healing stories in that Gospel with a focus on the wholeness of life, the healing ministry of Jesus, and the interactions between spiritual, physical, and mental health.

At each point, this study reaches beyond the study of Luke's healing stories into the present world of spiritual healing. The dynamic behind first century healings and those of our time is probably identical in principle, even if first century explanations differ from ours. We will study several aspects of this dynamic.

It is characteristic of our time that "respectable" mainline churches do not take the total healing ministry of the church seriously. We tend to separate spiritual matters from physical and to refer problems of physical health to the medical world. I intend in this study to give us a chance to reconsider this present practice and perhaps to revise it in the light of the ministry of Jesus as found in the Gospel of Luke.

In this book, the term "spiritual healing" stresses a healing dimension different from healing through medical and surgical procedures but one that is intimately related to it. I do not intend to set up tension between the two; both are needed.

I urge the reader to study carefully all the biblical passages on which the discussion is based. Different tranlsations will shed new light on these key passages, but I have chosen to quote from the Revised Standard Version as the one most widely used today. Among other versions, I recommend the New English Bible, the Jerusalem Bible, Today's English Version, and Clarence Jordan's paraphrase, the Cotton Patch Version.

I have scattered discussion questions, or questions to think about, throughout the text. Rather than gathering them together at the end of each chapter, I have added them at the most relevant places in little boxes.

My mood is intended to be informational, not judgmental. Many "unusual" ideas characterize the literature on spiritual healing. These ideas are sometimes based on inaccurate information or fail to consider all the data available. I have found it difficult to weed these out. Some readers may feel I need to do more weeding. I have intentionally risked being too inclusive rather than too exclusive to leave the reader more broadly informed.

After the introductory chapters on the Gospel of Luke and on the unity of religion and health, I have treated the principal factors in spiritual healing in separate chapters on "The Role of. . ." These factors are Faith, Touch, Prayer, the Word, and the Healer. In each of these chapters, the beginning point is drawn from those healing stories in Luke that emphasize that particular factor. Then we will examine the modern understanding(s) of that particular factor. After considering these individual factors, we will recognize the positive role that illness sometimes plays in our lives (in "The Role of Malady"). Here also the relevant parts of Luke begin the discussion. The next chapter, "Technique or Grace?" raises significant theological concerns which bear directly on the whole focus of the story. Chapter Ten brings the previous material together under the theme of wholeness, both individual and societal, and applies it to our regular church life. This chapter takes its base from Luke's healing stories.

A wise word from Francis MacNutt is appropriate for this study book. "Those who want simple answers and absolute clairty are bound to be disappointed. . . . There will always be a mystery."[1]

The three new chapters address two additional questions. In Chapter Eleven I go beyond the Gospel of Luke to report on what the rest of the New Testament says about healing.

I address the other question in Chapters Twelve and Thirteen. The earlier edition did not attempt to deal with spiritual healthiness.

---

[1]*Healing* (1974; rpt. New York: Bantam Books, 1980), p. 119.

1 Introduction to the Gospel According to Luke

Readings from Luke and Acts: Luke 1:1-4; Acts 1:1; Acts 24:2; Luke 24:13-53; Acts 1:3-8

What Is the Gospel of Luke?

The Gospel of Luke is the first half of a larger work. The second half of it is the New Testament† book we know as The Acts of the Apostles. Neither half of the work can be easily or fully understood apart from the other half. We will find it useful, therefore, to make some use of Acts, even though the center of our attention will be on Luke. Scholars often use the term Luke-Acts* to refer to the complete work.

The scope of Luke (volume I of Luke-Acts) is limited to the story of the earthly life of Jesus. It begins with events preparing for his birth and ends with his resurrection appearances. Acts (volume II) picks up where Luke ends and tells of the beginning of the church in Jerusalem and its expansion into the Hellenistic-Roman world. It ends with the preaching of Paul in the capital city of the empire—Rome itself.

---

*Words with an asterick can be found in the glossary at the back of the book.

---

†I use the traditional terms "Old Testament" and "New Testament" with some serious misgivings.

Especially since Jewish experience of the Holocaust in Hitler's Germany, we Christians have been forced to reexamine the implicit anti-semitic factors in our religion as a whole. The traditional designations of the two parts of our Bible as "Old" and "New" tends to reflect unfavorably on the first as inferior to the second. This implication is contrary to Christian orthodoxy, which affirms the full inspiration of the whole Bible.

At present, no alternative terminology seems better. André Lacocque

1

Why Was It Written?

In the preface to Luke (Luke 1:1-4), the author said that his purpose was to write an orderly and accurate account of the origin and early years of the Christian movement. He acknowledged some indebtedness to earlier accounts, and to eyewitnesses, and to ministers of the word. Also he reported that his study of these matters had been "for some time now." He stated that a primary purpose was to inform a person addressed as "most excellent Theophilos."* Either Theophilos was the name of a person otherwise unknown or a general term for any "friend of God." The presence of an honorific title makes it more likely that "Theophilos" was the name of a person in high public office, a Roman official like "most excellent Felix" of Acts 24:2.

Since the book was addressed to Theophilos, Luke placed special emphasis on the good relationship that the early Christian leaders had with Roman officials. Perhaps the emphasis was to inform Theophilos that the Romans who knew Jesus and Paul were friendly and supportive. At the most significant point, the execution of Jesus by the Romans, Luke reported that Pilate declared him innocent, three times, in fact, and placed the blame on the Jews. Some scholars guess that Roman persecution had already begun and that Luke's Gospel was defending the innocence of Christians.

But Luke also had another purpose: to add to the story a new body of teachings of Jesus. Many of the teachings, such as the Parable of the Prodigal Son (15:11-32) or the Parable of the Good Samaritan (Luke 10:33-37), are preserved only in Luke.

---

has proposed that we call the older part the "Prime Testament" (in *Biblical Studies*, L. Boadt, H. Cooner, and L. Klenicke, editors, p. 121). But that's "reverse discrimination" because "Prime" cannot be taken as the designation for the "Old Testament" without carrying with it implications of superiority. Paul van Buren has proposed "Hebrew Scriptures" for the Old Testament and "Apostolic Writings" for the New, but the Old Testament is partly in Aramaic, and "Scriptures" implies superiority over "Writings." "Hebrew" and "Greek" scriptures is closer to a good solution, but the needed new way has not yet emerged.

I will therefore, reluctantly, continue to use the traditional designation.

Still another purpose of Luke is closely related. His research led him to believe that some earlier writers were mistaken about some important points. He expanded their story and also corrected parts of it. All these earlier accounts ("many" according to Luke 1:1) have been lost, except one. Most scholars believe our Gospel of Mark was one of the earlier accounts. If this is true, then we can compare Mark with Luke and discover the parts of Mark that Luke believed were mistaken and therefore corrected. For example, Mark looks ahead to an appearance of the Risen Lord to the eleven disciples in Galilee (Mark 14:28 and 16:7), but in Luke the appearances are restricted to Jerusalem and Emmaus (Luke 24:49 and Acts 1:4). These differences help us understand the individual viewpoint of each of these Gospels and help clarify our understanding of the purposes of Luke.

When Was It Written?

Luke is not dated. Scholars usually guess that it was written late in the first Christian century, some time after Mark. Mark was written about the year 70 according to ancient tradition and modern scholarship. Scholarly guesses range from late in the first century to early in the second. The writer of Luke was not an eyewitness but belonged to the second generation of Christians according to the preface of the Gospel.

Who Wrote It?

Like all the other canonical Gospels, the third one is anonymous. Tradition has assigned the authorship to "Luke," who is mentioned as a companion of Paul in Colossians 4:14 and described in 2 Timothy 4:11 as the only one who remained with him to the end. In Colossians, Luke is called "the beloved physician." This tradition of authorship first appeared in a work of Irenaeus* around 185 C.E. (Common Era).*

This tradition has been accepted during most of the history of the church. Now, however, scholarship is divided about the accuracy of this tradition, largely because of serious discrepancies between Acts and Paul's major letters, Romans, Corinthians, and Galatians. If the physician Luke, companion of Paul, did not write it, we don't know who did. In this study we shall not argue for one side or the other of this quarrel; but, for convenience, we will continue to use the traditional name Luke to refer to the author.

Since Luke is written in excellent idiomatic Greek, rivaling the Epistle to the Hebrews as the best in the New Testament, it seems justified to assume that its author was well educated and belonged to the cultured upper classes. We might also assume that Luke was a converted Gentile, probably a Greek, rather than a Roman. Many Hellenistic Jews,* however, were fluent in literary Greek, so Luke may have been one of them. We cannot infer much about his cultural identity from his name; the Apostle Paul, for instance, was a Hellenistic Jew with the Roman name "Paulus."

The religious viewpoint expressed in Luke (see below) indicates that the author, whether a converted Gentile or a Hellenistic Jew, was quite "conservative" in his outlook. "Conservative" in the first century meant "more Jewish than Gentile." Luke was not nearly as "liberal" as Paul and did not share Paul's sense of freedom from the Law.

How Was It Written?

The author's preface (Luke 1:1-4) tells us that Luke was written after consulting the earlier written accounts, the traditions that came from the eyewitnesses, and the ministers of the word (early Christian preachers). He studied these sources "for some time past" (1:3) and then put the story in the order he believed was right, using his own judgment of what was accurate. He used research procedures familiar to us, under the inspiration of the Holy

Spirit, to produce his great two-volume work Luke-Acts.

Scholars have identified one of his principal sources as our Gospel of Mark, which was used also by the author of the Gospel of Matthew. Luke used Mark carefully, shortened some of the stories, and rewrote parts to improve the literary quality. To see both of these traits, compare Mark 5:21-43 with Luke 8:40-56. Luke also omitted parts of Mark. Luke quoted his sources accurately but sometimes added an explanation or comment that gives the reader a different impression. To see these traits, compare Mark 14:32-42 with Luke 22:39-46.

What Is Its Viewpoint?

Luke understood Christianity as the true form of the old religion; Christianity was the true Israel. The Gospel of Luke reveals that its author was loyal to the central tenets of Judaism. He knew the Hebrew scriptures well (but in their Greek translation). He began his Gospel with the scene of Zechariah in the Temple and ended it with the post-resurrection note that the followers of Jesus were "continually in the Temple, praising God." He treated Jerusalem with special veneration. Unlike the authors of Mark and Matthew, Luke took special pains to confine the resurrection appearances to the Holy City or nearby Emmaus. It was in Jerusalem that the church was born, with the coming of the Holy Spirit at Pentecost. According to Luke-Acts, the law of Moses was authoritative for Jesus (Luke 16:17), for Paul (Acts 21:24), and for Christianity in general.

Luke showed a special concern for the traditional forms of Jewish piety—prayer, fasting, and almsgiving. He had a decidedly Jewish view of the Holy Spirit (like that in the Hebrew scriptures). He also understood the powers of a healer in a specifically Jewish sense. (See pp. 54-56.)

Luke assumed a Jewish view of the oneness of the human body. Body, mind, and soul (spirit) are all aspects of a unity and are thoroughly interrelated. (See pp. 17-20.)

5

What Is Its Structure?

Following is an outline of the organization of Luke:

Chapter	Subject
1:1—2:52	Birth Stories of John and Jesus
3:1—4:13	Jesus' Baptism, Temptations The Beginnings of his Ministry
4:14—9:50	The Journey to Jerusalem
9:51—19:27	Luke's Special Section
19:28—23:56	The Passion Week
24:1-53	The Empty Tomb Resurrection Appearances

What Are Its Additional Concerns?

Luke showed a special interest in several topics. He mentioned prayer more frequently than the other Evangelists and emphasized the role of the Holy Spirit. Many scholars think Luke's emphasis on the Holy Spirit was intended to convince both Theophilos and his Christian readers that Christianity—the true Israel—was not a human movement but a divinely founded and guided religion.

He also gave a special place to the role of women in the life of Jesus and in the earliest history of the church.

Luke showed special interest in the ministry of healing. In the Gospel, he characteristically united the ministry of the word in preaching and teaching and the ministry of service to all the needs of human beings. Luke gave special emphasis to the holistic nature of Jesus' ministry and that of the apostolic church.

These special interests are in addition to Luke's main

purposes. Each of the main purposes and each of the special interests are excellent subjects for intensive study.

The Focus of This Study

This study-book has a definite focus. It does not attempt to study all the aspects of the Gospel of Luke. It does not even select the main purposes. Instead, it gives specialized attention to the holistic nature of Jesus' ministry and focuses on his concern for the healing of persons. We will note all the healing stories in Luke and relate these stories to the ministry of the church today. Following is a list of these stories and the chapter(s) in which they will be discussed in this book. Two references, however, are too general in nature to be helpful in this study (Nos. 20 and 21 in the list below).

This revised and expanded edition goes beyond the initial focus on the Gospel of Luke. It enlarges the data on healing to include the rest of the New Testament (Chapter Eleven). It also enlarges the holistic health concern to include the healthiness of our spiritual life, in addition to the more obvious healthiness of our body, our mind, and our emotions (Chapters Twelve and Thirteen).

The Healing Stories in Luke

Story	Luke	Text Chapter
1. Man with unclean demon	4:33-37	6, 10
2. Peter's mother-in-law	4:38-39	6, 10
3. Sick with various diseases	4:40-41	4
4. A leper	5:12-14	4, 5, 10
5. Multitudes	5:15-16	2, 4, 5, 10
6. Paralyzed man	5:17-26	6, 7, 8, 10
7. Man's withered hand	6:6-11	6, 10
8. Multitudes	6:17-19	4, 7, 8
9. Centurion's servant	7:1-10	2, 3, 6, 10
10. Widow's son	7:11-17	4, 10
11. Multitudes	7:18-23	10
12. Woman of the city	7:36-50	3
13. Gerasene demoniac	8:26-39	6, 7, 8, 10
14. Jairus' daughter	8:40-42, 49-56	4, 6, 10
15. Woman with flow of blood	8:43-48	3, 4, 7, 10
16. Multitudes	9:10-11	2, 7, 10
17. Child with convulsive spirit	9:37-43	5, 6, 7, 8
18. Man with a dumb demon	11:14-25	7, 8
19. Woman with spirit of infirmity	13:10-17	4, 6, 7, 10
20. Various persons	13:31-35	
21. Man with dropsy	14:1-6	
22. Ten lepers	17:11-18	7
23. Blind beggar	18:35-43	3, 6, 10
24. Slave's ear	22:47-53	4, 8

2 The Unity of Religion and Health

Readings from Luke: 4:16-21; 5:15; 9:1-2, 6, 11; 10:9, 29-37

Jesus' Holistic Ministry

Early in his ministry, Jesus returned to "Nazareth, where he had been brought up," entered the synagogue on the sabbath, and "stood up to read" (4:16). He was handed the Isaiah scroll. He turned the scroll until he came to the passage we have numbered as Isaiah 61:1-2. It is the great passage where the unknown prophet of post-exilic times announced that "the Spirit of the Lord" was upon him, anointing him (a Messianic phrase) to preach "good news" (another way of translating the Greek word for "gospel") to the poor.

The word "messiah" means "the anointed one." In Israel's national era 1020-586 B.C.E. (Before Common Era),* the king, who was anointed with oil by a religious authority, was regarded as "the anointed one" (Messiah). After the national era, there were no more kings. For a brief period in the last part of the second century B.C.E. and the first part of the first century B.C.E., the Jews in the Jerusalem area were independent and had their own Priest-King. After that, some Roman-appointed rulers, like Herod the Great, were given kingly status, but these kings were Roman agents.

Jews living under oppressive foreign rulers (Assyrians, Babylonians, Persians, Greeks, and Romans in that order) began to hope for, and believe in, a coming king who would restore their fortunes as a people. Thus arose "the Messianic hope" among the Jews. This development is fully explained in J. Klausner, *The Messianic Hope in Israel* (1955), and in S. Mowinckel, *He that Cometh* (1954).

9

Jesus claimed for himself this Isaiah passage with its reference to being anointed by the Spirit of the Lord. In this conception, however, the anointed one was not to be a ruling king but a proclaimer of the gospel ("good news") of God's concern for the poor, the captives, the blind, and the oppressed.

"The Spirit of the Lord is upon me,
because he has anointed me to preach good news to the poor.
He has sent me to proclaim release to the captives
and recovering of sight to the blind,
to set at liberty those who are oppressed,
to proclaim the acceptable year of the Lord." (4:18-19)

In applying this prophecy to himself, Jesus was announcing that his was not merely a preaching ministry. He was also anointed to heal and to bring release and freedom to the captives and the oppressed. This is a classic statement of a holistic view of ministry.

Luke had prepared the reader for this in the infancy stories. In the "Magnificat" of Mary (1:46-55), especially in verses 51-53, the holistic nature of Jesus' coming ministry is clearly predicted.

True to these declarations from Mary before Jesus was born and from Jesus at the very beginning of his ministry, Luke described the ministry of Jesus as fulfilling these bold claims. The people came to see Jesus—"to hear and to be healed" (5:15). When Jesus sent the Twelve on their mission, he sent them "to preach the Kingdom of God and to heal" (9:2). They received Jesus' instructions, and "went through the villages, preaching the gospel and healing everywhere" (9:6). When the Twelve returned, Jesus withdrew with them to Bethsaida, but the people discovered him. Jesus welcomed them and "spoke to them of the Kingdom of God and cured those who had need of healing" (9:11). Later, Jesus appointed seventy others and sent them out in teams of two. They were instructed to enter a town, "heal the sick in it and say to them 'the Kingdom of God has come near you'" (10:9).

Luke is the only Gospel that contains the Parable of the

Good Samaritan (10:29-37). This parable clearly teaches that discipleship is just as concerned with ministry to physical needs as it is with a spiritual witness.

We can see from Luke that religion and health went together in Luke's understanding of the ministry of Jesus. Jesus, the Great Evangelist, was also Jesus, the Great Physician. For the Christian, this is the the primary healing tradition from antiquity, the standard by which we should shape our practices today.

The Unity of Greek Medicine

In actual Christian history, another ancient healing tradition, the Greek, has been more influential than the Jewish tradition that Jesus exemplified. The Greek healing tradition has one of its roots in the mythology of Asklepios, the Greek healing-god. His cult gained popularity during the fourth century B.C.E. and spread to Rome early in the next century, where he was known as Aesculapius. In the earliest period of Christian history, Asklepios "was regarded by early Christians as the chief competitor of Christ because of his remarkable similarity in role and teachings to the Great Physician."[1] Shrines (sanctuaries) dedicated to Asklepios became famous healing centers all over the Hellenistic world. These were the principal hospitals of antiquity.

Like the Jewish healing tradition exemplified in Jesus, this Greek medical tradition treated the whole person, not just the physical aspect. This is evident in the operation of a sanitarium of Asklepios, such as the famous one at Epidauros or the one in Pergamum.

Cures had to be initiated by Asklepios who called the sick person to the healing center. This call was usually indicated by the appearance of a serpent (the chief symbol of Asklepios) in a dream. Upon arrival, the one desiring to be

[1]Darrel W. Amundsen and Gary B. Ferngren, *Health/Medicine and the Faith Traditions*, ed. Marty and Vaux (Philadelphia: Fortress Press, 1982), p. 80.

healed first went through a period of inner reflection, ridding himself or herself of all personal animosities toward others, confessing all wrongs, and removing guilt feelings. This was their method of purifying the mind and spirit. Then one waited for the summons into the sanctuary. This summons, like the initial call, was usually signified by the appearance of a serpent in a dream. When the priests were persuaded that the "patient" was invited into the sanctuary, he or she spent the night there, hoping for a sign of the god's presence and healing powers.

Many persons reported cures; many were not cured. Those who were cured usually left a votive tablet in the shrine recording their name, their ailment, and their cure. Excavators of these shrines have found hundreds of votive tablets.[2] All people who made the journey, whether cured or not, found the pilgrimage to be beneficial for their lives as a whole.

The impact of the Asklepios-tradition upon Christian civilization was deep and permanent. His symbol, the snake twined around a staff, is the standard symbol of the physician (Jewish and Christian alike). His two daughters, Panacea (cure-all) and Hygieia (health; hygiene) have become household words.

The Asklepian tradition of sleeping in sacred precincts (the *abaton*) to be healed is technically called "incubation."* Its roots go back to earlier Egyptian religion where ill persons slept in the tomb of Imhotep, Egypt's healing god. Even while Christianity was triumphing over this ancient religion, "incubation temples" remained popular throughout the Greco-Roman world. In fact, the custom was never abolished but "Christianized" and practiced in Christian churches. "In the Middle Ages, for instance, churches were sometimes equipped with mattresses and even baths for this purpose, a church in Cambridge [England] being particularly renowned for its incubation cures: and the practice is not yet extinct in the Greek Orthodox persuasion

---

[2]Many of these are transcribed and translated in Dr. Edgar J. Swift, *Jungle of the Mind*. Facsimile edition of 1931 publication. Essay Index Reprint.

and in certain corners of Roman Catholicism."[3]

In these earlier pre-modern days, both in the Asklepian Greek tradition and in medieval Christianity, "when medicine was bound up with religious ideas there was nothing to prevent the physician considering his patient [or the priest considering his parishioner] as a whole person."[4]

By way of contrast, the Hebrew tradition perceived the unity of religion and health apart from the priesthood. "There appears to be no evidence for priests functioning as physicians..." in the Hebrew scriptures.[5] Instead, the "healing" work of the priesthood is connected with the belief that illness is punishment for sin and cured by sacrificial rituals. (See the chapter on "The Role of Malady.") Spiritual healing is associated with the prophets (especially Elijah and Elisha), not with the priests. Jesus was a part of the prophet-healer tradition of Judaism.

Early Christian Traditions

Christianity arose in an atmosphere that was generally hostile. Suffering was accepted—almost expected—by many Christians. Because of the persecutions, strength to bear suffering was needed more than the healing emphasis characteristic of earlier apostolic times. (See the chapters on "The Role of Malady" and "Technique or Grace?")

After the persecutions were over, a late fourth century church leader Basil the Great wrote a tract on why Christians were still afflicted with illness. He listed six reasons. Illness, he wrote, might be:

1. sent by God as discipline to develop character.

2. sent by God as punishment for sin.

3. given to those God knows are strong enough to bear it as models for the weak.

4. sent to check one's sense of self-importance.

---

[3]Louis Rose, *Faith Healing*, revised from 1968 Gollancz edition (New York: Penguin Books, 1971), p. 25.

[4]Rose, p. 18.

[5]Darrell W. Amundsen and Gary B. Ferngren in Marty and Vaux, p. 65.

5. an affliction sent by Satan.

6. simply the result of poor nutrition or some similar natural cause.

Basil recommended consulting a physician when the illness was sent by God as discipline or when it was the result of natural causes. He made no recommendation for the other four causes.

The pattern illustrated in Basil is characteristic for most of the remainder of church history. When illness occurred:

> Some Christians relied exclusively on prayer, others combined secular medicine with prayer. Some resorted to secular medicine only when prayer proved ineffective, while others turned to prayer only when secular medicine did not avail. Some sought a more dramatic approach to divine intervention than prayer (e.g. faith healing, involving a variety of procedures) and had no recourse to physicians. Others sought such religious means only as a last resort after physicians have despaired. These different attitudes still exist side by side within Christianity and cults peripheral to it.[6]

The early church's recognition of "secular medicine" marked the beginnings of a separation between medicine and religion. Spiritual healing was on the decline in the mainstream of Christianity, and "secular medicine" was recognized as independent of the church.

Several practices developed in the Middle Ages which contributed to the decline of earlier forms of spiritual healing. Among these was an increasingly popular appeal to the saints for healing and especially to the curative powers of their relics. Sacramental healing gradually transformed the practice of "unction" (anointing the sick with oil to restore health as directed in James 5:14-15) into the Sacrament of Extreme Unction (anointing the dying for the salvation of their souls). The church also increasingly related the "mentally ill" to demon-possession.

The Loss of Holism in Protestantism

Protestant leaders, in their protests over non-scriptural

---

[6]Amundsen and Ferngren, p. 101.

Catholic practices, rejected relic-veneration healing, rejected the Sacrament of Extreme Unction, and pushed exorcism to the fringes of the church. John Calvin, for example,

> viewed medieval healing practices with disdain, ironically mocking the use of relics. Further, he held that the age of miracles was past, including healing by non-physical means, except by divine action. Calvin's more "modern" attitude toward health became a part of the tradition associated with his name [the Reformed Tradition].... Illness... was still often considered to be divine punishment or testing....[7]

These attitudes contributed to the separation of religion and physical health that is typical in modern Christianity. Most Christians today have driven a wedge between religion and health. Very few of us would consult our pastor about our health problems. Nor would we take our religious questions or problems to our local physician. The pastor's business is spiritual matters; the physician's is physical or mental health matters. In the words of Paul Tillich: "Theology and medicine lost the intimate connection they originally had, and always should have—for saving the person is healing him."[8]

Although it is generally true that this intimate connection has been lost, there are exceptions. We do have physicians and ministers who are consciously striving to be holistic in their practice. One conspicuous example of this is the Hospice Movement, which provides physical, psychological, social, and spiritual care for the ill. Other examples include the various holistic health associations and organizations like the Society of Teachers of Family Medicine. Nevertheless, a more specialized approach is still the prevailing one.

The root of this unfortunate separation lies in the rise of modern scientific medicine. This, in turn, roots back into

---

[7]James N. Lapsley, *Salvation and Health: The Interlocking Process of Life* (Philadelphia: Westminster, 1972), pp. 41-42.

[8]"The Impact of Psychotherapy on Theological Thought," *The Churches' Handbook for Spiritual Healing,* as cited by Lawrence W. Althouse in *Rediscovering the Gift of Healing* (Nashville: Abingdon, 1977), p. 50.

another tradition of Greek medicine, one associated with the name Hippocrates rather than Asklepios. Hippocrates, in the fifth century B.C.E. rebelled at the religious and priestly elements in the Asklepios cult. By treating health problems as almost exclusively physical, rooted in nature rather than in a divinity, he earned and deserves the title of "the father of (modern) medicine." He pioneered the unfortunate breakdown of the earlier holistic approach characteristic of the Asklepian hospitals of antiquity.

The Asklepian tradition was endorsed by Plato, the Hippocratic tradition by Aristotle. It seems that modern medicine has emphasized the tradition of Hippocrates while ignoring the history of healing recorded on the votive tablets of the temples of Asklepios. Plato complained that the greatest error of his day was the separation of the concept of the soul from that of the body in medical treatment.[9] Modern medicine and modern Christian ministry alike need to hear this complaint again.

The Recovery of Unity

We are now beginning to recover the more ancient awareness of the essential unity of the human person. We are indebted both to the Hebrew and the Greek traditions of healing in this rediscovery and its meaning.

One form of the modern recovery is found in psychosomatic medicine. This field of research and practice is named after two Greek words, *soma* (body) and *psyche* (the soul-mind-spirit-emotions complex). It recognizes the interrelations of the "physical" and the "non-physical" aspects of a human being. It is discovering that the "physical" is not merely physical, and that the "non-physical" is not merely non-physical. These two aspects are so integrated that mental health, spiritual health, emotional health, and physical health are all interrelated. When any one of these aspects of humanity is ill, that illness affects all the others.

But even psychosomatic medicine has paid more atten-

---

[9]Rose, p. 20.

tion to the mental and emotional aspects of the "non-physical" than to the spiritual. Recent attention to spiritual health is helping to make that correction.

Healing illness in full cooperation with physicians is also a major function of the church. Jesus Christ did not come to save souls only, or to save bodies only, but to save people.

Another form of modern recovery has developed out of the powerful impact of Mary Baker Eddy and Christian Science. She perceived the closest kind of unity between the body and the spirit (soul-mind). All healing, for all aspects of a human being, was under spiritual control, according to her. Spiritual healing, however, was the only recognized kind. Medical physicians were displaced by "practitioners."

Eddy claimed that bodily ailments have a spiritual cause. In many instances, this has been verified. She went further than most Christians have followed when she claimed that *all* physical illness is rooted in spiritual disorder. The truth in what she taught has helped to awaken a new sensitivity to the interrelations between body and spirit. In the words of the Christian Scientist Robert Peel: "The urgent need of our time is for a coherent view of life, at the same time religious and scientific...."[10]

In spite of its insight and its sensitizing value, Christian Science fails to convince most practicing Christians because they feel it claims too much. In the last analysis, Christian Science doesn't hold the body and spirit together in unity. It raises the spirit to the level of the only reality and ultimately denies the reality of the whole physical world, including our bodies.

The Wholeness of Life

To live by a concept of the wholeness of life is very difficult for most of us. William E. Phipps has observed that, "Until the psychosomatic integration of Jesus' personality is recognized, there is little hope for the recovery of holism by

---

[10]*Moving Mountains* (British Broadcasting Corporation, 1956), p. 4.

those who worship him and who think they should pattern their lives after his." He goes on to note that "Christians will probably be unable to deal wholesomely with their own human nature. They will either actively deny their bodily needs, or not fully integrate their beliefs with their real lives."[11]

Sam Keen has recently argued quite convincingly for what he calls "a resurrection of the bodily" in the spiritually dominant environment of the church. He notes that "Incarnation, if it is anything more than a once-upon-a-time story, means grace is carnal, healing is through the flesh." He adds that "the sacred must be rediscovered in what moves and touches us, in what makes us tremble...."[12] Our bodies and our souls are inseparable aspects of the whole person.

In the Hebrew tradition, a human being was a living *nephesh*—a body-soul unity. When his or her relationship to God was right, that person was in *shalom** (health-whole-ness-peace). In the early Christian Greek tradition, that right relationship was called *soteria** (salvation). We can see the Greek verb *sōzō* (the active aspect of the concept *soteria*) in its wider meaning in Luke 7:1-10. In verse three, the centurion asked Jesus to *diasōzē* (heal) his slave. He was not thinking about the spiritual condition of the slave but about his physical state. At the end of the story, in verse 10, the centurion returned to his house and found the slave *hygiainonta* (restored to health). *Sōzō* and *soteria* are here intimately linked with *hygiainō* (hygiene). Salvation means good health. *Shalom* and *soteria* include all dimensions of existences—the spiritual and physical, the individual and societal.

When one reflects on how this should affect the church's work in the world today, it is clear that our practice and our theology do not give much attention to the physical healing of persons and of society. Indeed, when the subject is raised

---

[11]*Recovering Biblical Sensuousness* (Philadelphia: Westminster, 1975), p. 158.

[12]Phipps, p. 158.

and human physical needs are brought up to the level of consciousness, we tend to get very uncomfortable and retreat into that dualism that leaves all of the individual physical health concerns to the physicians and the physical ills of society to the politicians, reserving for the church only spiritual health needs.

This attitude is especially typical of mainline Protestantism. Even in sectarian Protestantism, where the spiritual healing of personal physical ailments has remained a major concern of the Christian religion, there is often little or no awareness of the church's mission to society's illnesses. Personal physical healing by spiritual means tends to be "out-of-balance" with the rest of the Gospel. By the same standard, there is a sense in which mainline Protestantism has been off balance through its lack of attention to its role in physical health, both for the individual and society.

Through counseling and pastoral care, the churches have, in this century, done something to restore the fullness of the Gospel. But the inclusion of special attention to mental health problems is still very limited in most churches. If we fail to develop this more fully, then, as Howard Clinebell observes, "Mental health centers would then become the *de facto* churches in that they would be doing more to meet the growth and healing needs of persons than the churches."[13]

The churches are even more guilty when physical health problems are added to the concerns of the Christian mission. We refer most mental health problems and all physical health problems to specialists in those areas.

The wholeness which is broken by this specialization of spiritual and physical is illustrated by the etymology* of our English word "health." It comes from the Saxon word *hal*. From this root word, we have developed our word "hale," an almost obsolete word now surviving only in the popular phrase "hale and hearty," meaning in good health. From the same root comes our word "whole" and the commonest

---

[13]Howard Clinebell, ed., "Introduction," *Community Mental Health* (Nashville: Abingdon Press, 1970), p. 14.

greeting word "hello." Like *shalom,* "hello" is an expression wishing health and wholeness. Health and wholeness are thus etymologically bound together.

A recent study by Joseph H. Fichter investigates the spiritual dimension of health care. It asks the question, "Does modern medical practice take seriously the holistic approach to illness, which includes the spiritual as well as the physical, psychological, and social aspects of the human personality?" The "basic assumption" of the study is that "religion and spirituality are formally integrated with medicine and nursing not only in the... church-related hospitals but also in the pastoral-care departments" of non-church-related ones as well.[14]

"Formally" integrated, however, is not necessarily *practically* integrated. There is much to be done to bring about this needed integration.

We also need to broaden our definition of illness to include non-physical illnesses which do not seem to have an obvious effect on bodily health. They *do,* in fact, have an effect, and often a powerful one, but the connection often passes unnoticed:

> We are all handicapped, but some of us are handicapped in more immediately obvious ways. Who is to say, however, that a person twisted by an inability to love is less handicapped than someone crippled by polio? Who can say that someone blinded by jealousy is less handicapped than someone who has been physically blind from birth?[15]

One of the simplest and yet most effective ways of raising a congregation's level of consciousness of the unity of the mind-soul-spirit-emotions-body complex is through carefully planned worship experiences that exemplify this integration. Thomas and Sharon Neufer Emswiler have many helpful suggestions for doing this in their book *Wholeness in Worship.*

---

[14]*Religion and Pain: The Spiritual Dimension of Health Care* (New York: Crossroad, 1981), pp. 11-12.

[15]Thomas and Sharon Neufer Emswiler, *Wholeness in Worship* (New York: Harper and Row, 1980), p. 46.

3 The Role of Faith

Readings from Luke: 7:1-10, 36-50; 8:43-48; 17:5-6; 18:35-43

The Healings of Jesus

In two famous healing stories found only in Luke, Jesus stressed the role of faith as the key to the healing. Two others shared with Matthew and Mark make the same emphasis. In the first of these four, Jesus heals the slave of a centurion by a word spoken *in absentia* and then gives the centurion higher praise for his faith than any of those "in Israel." This is only an implicit affirmation of the role of faith in the healings of Jesus, but it seems justifiable to include it as an example of faith.

In your opinion, what place does faith play in the healings done by (or through) Jesus?

The second story, also unique to Luke, contains Jesus' famous pronouncement to the woman of the city, "your faith has saved you; go in peace" (7:50). This story also involves the role of sin and repentance, which we'll examine in the chapter "The Role of Malady." The related stories in Mark 14:3-9, Matthew 26:6-13, and John 12:1-8 all make quite a different point and do not mention a faith dimension at all.

The same message, in exactly the same words (in Greek), appears in the story of the woman with the flow of blood

(Luke 8:43-48). This story is found also in Mark (Luke's probable source) and in Matthew. In Mark, the phrase is slightly different in the Greek text, though the Revised Standard version obscures this difference by giving the English version an identity not present in the Greek. Mark's text says "your faith has saved you; go your way in peace" (Mark 5:34). Matthew has only "your faith has saved you" (Matthew 9:22).

In the story of the healing of the blind beggar at Jericho, Jesus says again "your faith has saved you" (Luke 18:42). His probable source Mark, who says the beggar's name is Bartimaeus, uses the same words, prefaced by, "Go your way" (Mark 10;52). This is the same preface-phrase that Mark used earlier in 5:34. Matthew not only replaces Bartimaeus by two blind men but also makes the healing effective by the touch of Jesus, leaving out the faith statement altogether (Matthew 20:29-34).

The key phrase, then, is reported four times in Luke, twice in Mark, and only once in Matthew. In all the quotations above, I have translated the Greek phrase literally "your faith has *saved* you." The Revised Standard Version translates it literally only once (in Luke 7:50). In all the others, it is translated "your faith has *made you well*." This is a legitimate option, because the verb (*sōzō*) has both meanings: it usually means to save or rescue or deliver from some danger and therefore was used also to mean to heal or to cure. The word itself, as shown above on p. 18, illustrates the unity of religion and health.

How do the two translations ("saved" or "made well") illustrate the unity of religion and health?

Luke reports 24 episodes about Jesus' healing activities. Of these, eighteen are about specific individuals and six are general references to healings. Of the specific individual healings, faith is a significant factor in eight. Of course, it can be assumed to be present in many others, perhaps in most of them. But one could also assume that Jesus healed by touch even when the touching is not mentioned, and so on for each factor. That faith is an important element is beyond question, but just *how* important is it?

The term "faith-healing" puts an exaggerated emphasis on the role of faith in healing. Typical of many of those deeply involved in the healing ministry of the church, Francis MacNutt begins his discussion on "The Faith to Be Healed" with the too-strong statement: "All the books on healing—including *the* book on healing, the New Testament—emphasize the role that faith plays in healing. 'Go in peace, your faith has made you whole," is a constant saying of Jesus.'[1] I have no quarrel with the translation "whole," rather than "made well" or "saved," because the verb means all those things; but, since this pronouncement of Jesus occurs in only four stories, and exactly like that in only two of them, it is hardly justifiable to describe it as "a constant saying of Jesus." Let's acknowledge, then, that, in one-third of the healing reports in Luke, Jesus heals in the presence of explicit faith. In all the others, either different factors are emphasized, or no factor is mentioned.

Whose Faith Is Needed?

In four of the faith-healings in Luke, it is the faith of the healed person which activates the healing (and in one of these, the account in another Gospel omits the faith dimension: Matthew 20:29-34).

Another faith-healing calls special attention to the faith of the centurion; he was neither the healer nor the one healed but a "third party" (a general name for one who is neither the healer nor the recipient.) Is this story telling us that in some way "third party faith" can be effective in healing?

---

[1]MacNutt, p. 99.

> Do you believe that faith is essential on the part of persons who need to be healed? Why or why not?
>
> Who needs to have faith—the healer or the one healed, or someone else? Any one of them? Is it more effective if all three are present? Are two better than one?

Although Luke has no healing stories that emphasize the role of the healer's faith, the larger evidence makes it mandatory to include this as another dimension. Luke does stress the power of faith in the teachings of Jesus. Once the disciples came to Jesus with the request that he "increase their faith" (17:5-6). Although he did not respond to their plea, he made a strong statement about the power of faith: a tiny amount (like a grain of mustard seed) is sufficient to uproot a sycamore tree and plant it in the sea. This refers to the power of faith in the healer, rather than the healed person, but it could apply also to the faith of the third party.

Perhaps a caution is in order here to help keep our thinking straight. We all tend to read factors into the data that we think should (or must) be there, even though unmentioned. When we do this, our pre-conceptions govern our use of the data. Werner Heisenberg, in his *Physics and Beyond*, reports that Albert Einstein once said to him: "It is the theory which decides what we can observe."[2] Mary Baker Eddy made a similar statement in her *Science and Health*. She said, "Mortal mind sees what it believes as certainly as it believes what it sees."[3] For example, if one is already convinced that faith on the part of the one who needs healing is an essential, then one will assume that faith in all instances of spiritual healing and explain all failures as

---

[2] (New York: Harper and Row, 1971), p. 63.

The larger context of the quotation is "...It may be heuristically useful to keep in mind what one has actually observed. But on principle, it is quite wrong to try founding a theory on observable magnitudes alone. In reality the very opposite happens. It is the theory which decides what we can observe."

[3] (Boston: The First Church, 1906), p. 86, lines 29-30.

24

due to a lack of faith. And so it goes with each other element in this mysterious realm.

Different Concepts of Faith

Whether on the part of the first party (the healer), the second party (the one who is healed) or the third party (anyone else), faith is commonly understood as trust, belief, confidence, and hope, combined in one powerful attitude. This faith can be in God's power to intervene in a special way, or in some "immutable laws" of God that govern health. (See the chapter "Technique or Grace.")

This faith is often augmented by "imaging" the final result. "Imaging" is more powerful than "imagining" the desired result. It is more like seeing the forthcoming results ahead of time. Just *how* imaging helps is not explained in the same ways by those who advocate it or those who have experienced its benefits. For some,[4] it is the calling out of the powers of the subconscious mind, with its link to Infinite Power. With others it is a kind of psychic pre-cognition, partly, but not wholly, involving the human will. For still others it is one way to create and maintain a positive attitude that in itself is a factor in the healing process.

Do you know of an example in your own experience of someone who has been helped by "imaging" the final result?

Others experience faith as a close and intimate relationship with God (or Christ or the Holy Spirit). This is a relationship of acceptance (God's acceptance of us) and inner transformation, freely given to unworthy persons. It is the kind of faith that many believe Paul was trying to proclaim—faith as a gift of God—a newly-given acceptance

---

[4]Joseph Murphy, *The Power of Your Subconscious Mind* (1963; rpt. Englewood Cliffs, New Jersey: Prentice-Hall, 1981), p. 76.

of sinners and an indwelling spirit to transform the sinner into the image of Christ.

For many persons "faith" means "*the* faith." It means having the correct doctrines. John Sanford describes this faith as "... a total acceptance of a religious system.... The person who is able to accept all that is offered to him with little or no doubt, is a faithful member."[5]

It is easy to confuse faith with optimism. Paul Tournier reflects on his own experience with this tendency:

> I am by nature optimistic, whereas my wife is pessimistic. I am confident, she is apprehensive. For a long time I reproached her for her pessimism as indicating a lack of faith. For my own part I prided myself on my optimistic outlook as if it came from my faith and not from my inborn disposition. One day, when we both had a great act of faith to perform, I realized during my quiet time that I was being less than honest in confusing faith with optimism, to my own advantage. The truth was that real faith was as difficult for me as it was for my wife.[6]

Another way to approach the meaning of faith is to look at its opposite, "fear." "Fear," Robert Leslie observes:

> is probably the most common and subtle of diseases. Fear can affect virtually every organ of the body.... Fear invites illness.... *Faith is the opposite of fear.* Faith has a transforming and healing power that literally achieves miracles. When cures of serious organic diseases occur without medical intervention, researchers often find that strong faith has been at work.[7]

He notes that one can describe the whole ministry of Jesus as one of deliverance from fear. "Do not be afraid" is a phrase Jesus used frequently. "Jesus' answer for fear was always the same," Leslie maintains, "Fear is overcome by faith..."[8] (2 Timothy 1:7).

---

[5]John Sanford, *Healing and Wholeness* (New York: Paulist Press, 1977), p. 11.

[6]Paul Tournier, *The Healing of Persons,* translated by Edwin Hudson (New York: Harper and Row, 1965), pp. 79-80.

[7]Robert Leslie, *Health, Healing and Holiness* (Nashville: Graded Press, 1971), p. 39.

[8]Leslie, p. 39.

> Can you give examples of how fears are overcome by faith?

Is Faith Essential?

The role that faith plays in health is clearly positive, but is it essential? If so, what *kind* of faith is essential?

Contrary to common assumptions, faith on the part of the ill person cannot be regarded as essential. No one doubts its beneficial values, but an essential—a "without which not" (*sine qua non*)—it isn't. This is clearly demonstrated in those genuine healings where the one who is healed is not a person of faith. Atheists have been healed. Skeptics of the whole process of spiritual healings, including those who don't believe in the healer's healing powers, have been spiritually healed. When a man came to Mrs. Worrall for healing and first confessed that he was an atheist and had no faith, she told him not to worry; she had enough faith for both.[9]

Probably the most convincing reason for thinking that the faith of the healed person is not essential comes from the spiritual healing of animals and plants. (See pp. 33-34.) It is very difficult to attribute anything like faith—in any of the popular senses—to animals or plants.

Not only is faith on the part of the one who is healed not essential; neither is faith on the part of the healer. The faith of the third party is made non-essential by the many instances of healing where there is no third party.

But to recognize that faith is a non-essential to the whole process of spiritual healing is not to deny that faith is often a powerful factor. Faith can even be *the crucial factor* in some healings. Faith, in all of its meanings and in all three parties, is always a positive element in the healing process. But the

---

[9]Joyce Hopkins, "Miracle of Healing...," *United Methodist Reporter* (May 1, 1981), p. 3.

process is more mysterious than we can explain, at least at the present time. In the realistic summary of Francis MacNutt, Faith "is often—but not always—a precondition for healing."[10] Or again, "The faith needed for healing can be in anyone—or no one."[11]

Faith Is a Gift

Whether faith is trust or a personal relationship with God, it is important to emphasize again that "it is not our own doing; it is the gift of God" (Ephesians 2:8). Striving to achieve faith is a fruitless struggle. It reminds Francis MacNutt of:

> what often happens when I begin to lose a tennis game. I start overstraining; I hit the ball harder, trying to make winning shots in order to regain my confidence; I smash my serve harder to make a few quick, impressive aces. But all that really happens is that I hit the ball out of court more often, and I begin missing my first serve. My straining efforts worsen my game.... I only end up beating myself.[12]

He goes on, "...I am trying to create faith in myself, forgetting that faith is a gift from God."[13]

Again and again, the deeper answer of mainstream Christianity patiently explains how faith comes. It is not an achievement but a work of grace. We can put ourselves in the means of grace and then wait in patience while remaining active in our service to others in response to grace already achieved. (See the chapter "Technique or Grace?" for further explanations of "grace.")

---

[10]MacNutt, p. 105.
[11]MacNutt, p. 116.
[12]MacNutt, pp. 107-108.
[13]MacNutt, p. 109.

4 The Role of Touch

Readings from Luke: 4:40; 5:12-16; 6:17-19; 7:11-17; 8:40-56; 13:10-17; 22:47-53

How Jesus Used Touch

In Luke the ministry of Jesus clearly begins on the theme of Jesus' healing activity. After several specific healings described in chapter four, there is a general statement, "all those who had any that were sick with various diseases brought them to him" (4:40). Then the summary statement goes on to say that "he laid his hands on every one of them and healed them" (4:40).

Healing by "laying on of hands" is characteristic of Jesus, especially in Luke. Once when approached by a leper who asked to be healed, Jesus "stretched out his hand, and touched him" (5:13), telling him that he would be clean. The story reports that the leprosy left him "immediately" (5:13).

On another occasion, after spending an entire night in prayer, Jesus was the center of another multitude which had come from Judea and Jerusalem and the seacoast of Tyre and Sidon. He cured those who were demon-possessed, and then the account reports that "all the crowd sought to touch him, for power came forth from him and healed them all" (6:19).

One of the most amazing of the "touching stories" in Luke is the one that tells about Jesus encountering a procession carrying a dead man out of the city of Nain. It was accompanied by the dead man's mother, a widow. He was her only son. Jesus saw her weeping, "had compassion on her," and touched the bier carrying the dead man. The procession halted. Then Jesus told the young man to rise up and he did so, talking as he sat up (7:11-15). Here Jesus did not touch the man directly but only the bier.

Two stories are combined in another account. One story is begun only to be interrupted by another. Then the first one is completed. In both of them, touching is an important element. The first story tells of a dying girl, only twelve years old, who was restored to health when Jesus took her by the hand and told her to arise. The second is an even more dramatic instance of the power of touching. In it a woman who had "a flow of blood" for twelve years came through the crowd and touched "the fringe of his garment" and was immediately healed. Here the touch was indirectly made, rather than skin to skin.[1]

Another instance of Jesus healing by the "laying on of hands" is in the story of the bent over woman: "Now he was teaching in one of the synagogues on the sabbath. And there was a woman who had had a spirit of infirmity for eighteen years; she was bent over and could not fully straighten herself. And when Jesus saw her, he called her and said to her, "'Woman, you are freed from your infirmity'" (13:10-12). She could not stand up straight until Jesus laid his hands on her and "immediately she was made straight" (13:13).

When Jesus was arrested in the garden of Gethsemane, one of his disciples (identified as Peter in John 18:10) drew his sword and cut off the ear (the right ear in John) of the slave of the High Priest (identified as "Malchus" in John). Jesus immediately responded, "'No more of this!'" Then "he touched his ear and healed him" (22:51).

In every case except one, Jesus is described as using his hands to heal, healing by touching. In the other case, a woman seeking healing touched his garment.

Touching was by no means unique with Jesus. The Apostles healed by touch (Acts 19:11-12): "And God did extraordinary miracles by the hands of Paul, so that

---

[1]Note the interesting parallel in Acts 19:11-12. Note also that Matthew (9:18-26) associates the healing with Jesus' words rather than the woman's touch. In both accounts the woman's faith is lifted up as important.

handkerchiefs or aprons were carried away from his body to the sick, and diseases left them and the evil spirits came out of them." It was a common healing method in ancient times and has continued to be practiced ever since.

> What is the attitude toward healing by touch in your local church? What has contributed to this point of view?

Neither has it been limited to Mediterranean or European culture. Healing by touch is portrayed in cave drawings as early as 15,000 years ago and is mentioned in the earliest examples of writing. It is common in India, China, Tibet and elsewhere in the Orient. It is a universal process that is equally present in the healing activities of all cultures.

The Healer as Agent

Precisely how touching sometimes heals is still not known. In both the past and the present, it is often explained in terms of supernatural power expressing itself through the human healer. Since healing is usually viewed as "good," the supernatural power was regarded as "good" also. That is, a good god was the real healer. In Jewish experience, this power was "Yahveh." In Christian experience, it was Christ. In other religions, it was another supernatural power by another name.

For those Christians who are provincial in their own religion, the existence of healings by touch in non-Christian settings becomes a serious theological problem. Such Christians tend either to be skeptical of the reality of such healings or to assign them to Satan, as was done by Christians in the late Middle Ages in Europe and is done among some fundamentalists today,. Satan doing good? Yes, they say, but with a bad motive—namely, to lead away the faithful into heresy or apostasy.*

The traditional Christian explanation that it is Christ

31

healing through the touch of a human stems from the earliest traditions of Christianity. Acts reports both Peter (3:6) and Paul (16:18) healing "in the name of Jesus." Similarly a modern healer-by-touch, Oskar Estebany, a devout Roman Catholic from Hungary, "when pressed..., would say he felt he was a channel for the spirit of Jesus the Christ."[2]

Other modern Christian healers usually say the same thing. Well-known Protestant healers Olga Worrall of the New Life Clinic at Mt. Washington United Methodist Church in Baltimore, Maryland, and Agnes Sanford, who lives in California, agree. They illustrate the traditional "in house" explanation of the healing powers of touching. These Christian explanations are like those of other religions, each believing that its special way of grasping the reality of the divine presence is the secret of the healing touch.

Has your local church had a healing service? If so, what was it like?

A Modern Alternative

Contemporary research is moving in new directions. Most of it is very recent. All of it is in the present century. More research is needed before we can draw any sound conclusions. In the research data we now have, it does appear that touching itself is not the source of healing. The person who is doing the touching seems to be the clue to the healing powers of touching. The healer is the source of the healing touch. ("The Role of the Healer" will be discussed in a separate chapter.)

Controlled touching experiments demonstrate that the touch of certain persons is more effective in healing than

---

[2]Dolores Krieger, *The Therapeutic Touch* (Englewood Cliffs, New Jersey: Prentice-Hall, Inc, 1979), p. 6.

touches from randomly chosen persons. The experiments are most informative when the maladies are not in human subjects but in animals, or even plants. Oskar Estebany discovered his healing power when he was able to heal horses in the Austrian cavalry. People then brought their ill pets, and he healed some of these. Afterward he began to use his gift to benefit humans and has continued to help humans ever since.

Have you personally experienced healing through touch? in a religious setting? in another setting? Describe the healing.

Touch experiments that use animals or plants as subjects have certain advantages over those that use human subjects. Humans are endowed with imagination and preconceptions that may invalidate, or at least complicate, the experiment. Animals are not as subject to suggestion and can be presumed to have no expectations that might affect the results. Plants are even more "objective" subjects.

Currently, most healers are reluctant to "waste" their powers on animals or plants when humans are in need. In addition, while many healers are dedicated and devoted to their work, they may not be scientifically minded and may not recognize the need for controlled experiments and genuine research.

Bernard Grad of McGill University in Toronto has experimented with healing animals by touch. A healer, identified only as "Mr. X," proved to be of real help in healing experimentally wounded mice. When other persons touched the mice in controlled settings, their touches were found to be insignificant in the healing process. Grad separated the wounded mice into two groups. The cages for the two groups were identical. One group was treated medically and handled by persons with no claim to be healers. The other group was also treated medically, but not handled by anyone. Mr. X put his hands on some of the cages. The results? Handling by non-healers had no measurable effect on the healing process. But the mice in the cages which Mr. X touched healed more rapidly than the others.[3]

With the virtual elimination of preconceptions, expectations, and faith elements in healing in subjects such as these mice, the source of the healing powers of the touch of some persons seems to lie in the healer. But more experimentation is needed to test these indications.

Informal Touching

There is another dimension of touching in the process of becoming well-healthy-whole. It is related to the formal laying on of hands, but it is not the same. (Perhaps it is only a difference in degree.) This is the informal kind of touching that is the most basic of all human encounters—the skin-to-skin encounter. According to Sidney Simon, "...all of us have a basic skin hunger much like our physical appetite. We need touch as much as we need food. When we don't get it, something inside us withers."[4]

Much more generalized data comes from recent research on the beneficial effects of touching without reference to a recognized healer and with no association with the more formal ritualistic "laying on of hands." According to an article by Sherry Cohen, Emanuel Chusid, who is the Medical Director of the Westchester County Medical Center in New York, reports that a child who has Down's Syndrome will walk earlier if he or she gets a lot of hugging, touching, and stroking from his or her mother. She also reports that physicians at the Harvard Medical School treat cerebral palsy victims with a special touching technique that seems to be effective in reducing spasms and enabling more normal muscle action. Sick babies at the Rainbow Babies and Children's Hospital of Case Western Reserve University in Cleveland are helped when they are touched, held,

---

[3]See the *International Journal of Parapsychology*, Spring 1961, for a complete report of these experiments.

[4]T. and S. Emswiler, p. 18.

and stroked regularly by volunteers. Untouched babies develop *marasmus* (wasting away), according to several studies.[5]

The healing—"whole-ing"—aspect of this kind of touch is thought by some to be the ingredient of love expressed in the touching. Touching is love and care and concern made physical and physically felt. Sidney M. Jourard has pointed out that when a person reaches out and touches another, she or he is saying, "I want to share; I want to help." And when the other permits or welcomes the touch, allowing his or her "space" to be invaded, this other is replying, "I want to share; I want to be helped."[6] Or, as the Emswilers put it, "touch is the language of love."[7]

How do you feel about touching people? About being touched? Describe a time when someone reached out to you by touching.

How could touching be incorporated into a worship service in a comfortable, helpful way?

A persistent problem that arises when touching is encouraged is the "taboo" in our culture about touching. For some people, touching is regarded primarily as a sexual gesture. We usually apologize if we accidently touch someone—especially a stranger—as if to say, "I didn't mean anything by it." Even joining hands in a worship service setting makes some persons uncomfortable.

This discomfort stems partly from the issue of not having given permission to be touched. Touching threatens our privacy and may provoke a feeling of being manipulated. But deeper than that, the taboo against touching is probably

---

[5]Sherry Suib Cohen, "The Amazing Power of Touch," *Ladies Home Journal* (June 1982), p. 110. Many other accounts of the benefits of generalized touching are given in Ashley Montagu's book *Touching: The Human Significance of the Skin* (New York: Columbia University Press, 1971).

[6]Krieger, p. 82.

[7]T. and S. Emswiler, p. 19.

grounded in Victorian sexual attitudes. Basic in positive human relationships is a healthy appreciation of touching as a non-sexual expression of love and concern.

Laying on of Hands

A yet different insight into the value of touch goes back to a different use of the more formal "laying on of hands." This time it is not to heal but to transmit special spiritual power to another. In Acts, for instance, Simon "the Great" saw Peter and John giving baptized Samaritans the power of the Holy Spirit by the laying on of hands. "Now when Simon saw that the Spirit was given through the laying on of the apostles' hands," he tried (unsuccessfully) to buy this power for himself (Acts 8:9-24). This transfer of power was given to the Seven (Acts 6:6) and to Barnabas and Saul (Acts 13:3) for their respective jobs in the early church.

The practice of laying on of hands is very ancient and is found in many cultures. In primitive societies, it transmits "power" (*mana*). In the ancient Hebrew tradition, it anointed a king with the Spirit of Yahveh (1 Samuel 16:13-14). In Christian tradition it is called "ordination" or "commissioning."

Is there a connection between the *healing* power of laying on of hands and its *ordaining* power?

5 The Role of Prayer

Readings from Luke: 5:12-16; 6:12; 9:28-36; 11:1-13; 18:1-14; 19:45-46

How Jesus Used Prayer

Prayer is one of the special themes in Luke. Luke, more than the other Evangelists, emphasized Jesus' prayer practices.

Luke mentions a number of times that Jesus prayed. For instance, Jesus once healed a leper. This event drew crowds of people who came "to hear and to be healed" (5:15), but Jesus chose to withdraw into the wilderness and pray. One must suppose from this that prayer was an essential element in the ministry of Jesus. In another place, Jesus "went out into the hills to pray; and all night he continued in prayer to God" (6:12). The next time he did this, he took Peter, John, and James with him. As they watched him pray, he was transformed before them, and they experienced a vision of Moses and Elijah with him (9:28-36).

In his teaching, Jesus stressed the importance of prayer. Two parables (found only in Luke) illustrate this. One is at the beginning of chapter 11, the other at the beginning of chapter 18.

The first one follows immediately after Luke's version of what we call "the Lord's Prayer" (the version in Matthew 6:9-13 is the more familiar):

> "Father, hallowed be thy name. Thy kingdom come. Give us each day our daily bread; and forgive us our sins, for we ourselves forgive every one who is indebted to us; and lead us not into temptation" (Luke 11:2-4).

37

Christians have used this as the model prayer ever since.

The brief appeal, "thy Kingdom come," and the petition, "Give us each day our daily bread," extend the concerns of the prayer beyond private and personal needs. In the sense that God's work is accomplished through human agents and in the faith that the Church is God's means of carrying out the divine mission, we are responsible for the establishment of the Kingdom and the supplying of that daily bread. Prayer, for Jesus, was never a substitute for action but rather the dynamic for action.

The parable following the Lord's Prayer (11:5-13) describes how an inconvenienced neighbor will eventually respond to a persistent call for help. The parallel parable (18:1-8) tells how an unjust judge will finally give justice just to be rid of the plaintiff. Both parables teach persistence, and both contrast God with the reluctant neighbor and with the unjust judge.

In the famous incident described in all four Gospels where Jesus drove out the money-changers from the Temple, Jesus quoted from Isaiah 56:7 that the Temple is a "house of prayer" (19:45-46).

We know that prayer was an important aspect of Jesus' life. But nowhere did Luke record that Jesus prayed in direct connection with a healing session.

In his second volume (our Acts), Luke recorded many acts of healing by the apostles, but in these accounts prayer is mentioned only once. In the story of Peter raising Tabitha from the dead (Acts 9:36-41), "Peter first sent everyone out of the room and then he knelt down and prayed...." (Acts 9:40). No further explanation is given.

What Is Prayer?

In subsequent history, however, prayers are both common and theologically sound. These include personal prayers for our own healing and intercessory prayers for the healing of others. Many of these have been formally structured into the liturgy. Many more are spontaneous cries for help.

The *power* of prayer is too well-attested to be doubted. The explanation of that power, however, is something else. There are many explanations, many "definitions," and many strange and wonderful ideas. A basic need of our time is to understand prayer better. Mary Baker Eddy, almost a century ago, spoke for today when she declared that "prayer may be a far more important field for research than neutron kinetics."[1] (Now we would say "nuclear physics.")

How important do you think prayer is in healing? Why?

What *is* prayer? How does it function in healing? *Why* should we pray? *How* should we pray?

Prayer is commonly understood as talking with God. It includes all kinds of talking—praise, thanksgiving, confession, petition, intercession, and dedication. Sometimes it invokes complaints and bitterness, and disappointments. In fact, it may include any kind of talk.

Prayer is also understood as meditation or contemplation. In this prayer, conscious words are not dominant, but feelings and introspective silence become prominent. Silence, quiet, relaxation, deep breathing, trying to be receptive to the meaning of God's presence—these constitute prayer for many persons. This prayer is more listening than talking, and it often complements the talking-type prayer in a real attempt to make prayer a two-way conversation.

For others, prayer is a life-style. It includes and involves action, actually living religious convictions. It may or may not include the more typical prayer definitions. For this action-oriented prayer, all of life is a prayer.

---

[1] "Message to the Mother Church for 1901," p. 1.

How We Pray

When prayer is related to health, and wholeness, and healing, it is quickly apparent that some prior concept of health processes determines (or at least influences) how prayer relates. For instance, if one shares the ideas of Oskar Estebany, Olga Worrall, or Kathryn Kuhlman—that they are simply agents for the power of God or Christ or the Holy Spirit—then prayers of petition and intercession are basic to the healing process. Healing is a work of grace. If one shares the ideas of Ambrose Worrall, John Sanford, or Joseph Murphy—that health matters follow strict laws—then the appropriate prayers are requests for a better grasp of the healing laws rather than a divine intervention.

How do your own beliefs affect your prayers for healing? Write a prayer for healing based on your personal beliefs.

From some perspectives, prayer is less important to the healing process. If one believes the healer's power is somehow in himself or herself, then prayer in the conventional sense is not important. As one dips more deeply into the psychic aspects of health, prayer becomes less relevant also. Or prayers for physical health may be ruled out on "dispensational" grounds. Many Protestants believe that the healing miracles of Jesus and the early church were a special "dispensation" for the Apostolic Age and do not happen in our time. John Calvin, for instance, "emphasized strongly praying only within the bounds set by the Lord's Prayer, which makes no mention of healing as such."[2] Some modern evangelicals and liberals alike share this dispensational view.

Responses from a congregation of Christians will include several points of view on all these matters. Prayer in such a

---

[2]James N. Lapsley, *Salvation and Health*, p. 45. From *The Institutes of the Christian Religion*, Beveridge edition, Vol. II, p. 198.

corporate setting may have to be more diffused and general. For instance, all would agree that God favors health. As expressed by Steve Land, "It is always God's will to heal, but to heal the whole person and the whole creation according to God's own timetable."[3]

We can pray "in the firm conviction that our prayers make a difference," the Emswilers remind us. They continue:

> We are not saying that a gathered community's prayers can always bring exactly what we think we want, but such prayers can help to bring healing and new understanding, no matter what the outcome of the particular crisis, and we have seen these prayers transform the outcome.[4]

Group Prayer

George MacLeod also helps us to see the broader values of prayer, regardless of one's personal views on health. He notes that corporate prayer includes: "Prayers of confession for our own inadequacies, of active acceptance of our forgiveness.... Prayer is also always made for doctors, nurses, and all who, with us, are God's instruments of healing."[5] "Authentic prayer," the Emswilers remind us, "almost always impels us to action. Prayer is dangerous to someone who doesn't want to get involved."[6]

These prayer-values make it plain that, regardless of how one views the mystery of health, corporate praying is a valuable experience. Prayer taps into a powerful force.

Experimental Prayer

Some persons believe that prayer-power can be understood through experiments. This belief is held by some

---

[3]Barbara McYahee Brown quoting Steve Land in *Ministry and Mission*, III, No. 3 (September 1978), pp. 4-5.

[4]T. and S. Emswiler, p. 53.

[5]*The Place of Healing in the Ministry of the Church* (Glasgow, Scotland: The Iona Community Publishing Department), p. 3.

[6]T. and S. Emswiler, p. 52.

scientists like Ambrose Worrall (physical science) or Anton Boisen (psychology and medicine). It is also promoted by some non-scientific healers such as Agnes Sanford. Boisen, for instance, believed that the role of religion in illness and health was poorly understood. Furthermore, it would never be understood properly until it had been "studied thoroughly by a sympathetic investigator."[7] This study would be an empirical study, based on controlled conditions.

Ambrose Worrall, who confessed to being "skeptical by nature"[8] favored "the scientific approach to all phenomena." He thought that "we should seek, by the scientific approach, to understand, to learn the laws governing spiritual healing."[9]

Agnes Sanford, a healer but not a scientist, proposes a "simple," "childlike" method, experimental in nature, and thus allies herself with the prayer experimenters: "One decides upon a definite subject for prayer, prays about it and then decides whether or not the prayer-project succeeds. If it does not succeed, one seeks a better adjustment with God and tries again."[10]

Since Agnes Sanford is also committed to laws governing health, her experimental prayers are necessarily petitionary or intercessory. If prayer fails, then there must have been a flaw (or flaws) in the process. We slowly learn the laws by experimentation, and as we conform more closely, results improve. She uses this analogy to clarify her viewpoint: if one turns on an electric lamp and it fails to shine, one does not say "'There is no electricity!'" One says instead, "'There is something wrong with this lamp.'"[11]

---

[7]Hugh W. Sanborn, *Mental-Spiritual Health Models: An Analysis of the Models of Boisen, Hiltner and Clinebell* (Washington: University Press of America, 1979), p. 38.

[8]Ambrose Worrall, *The Gift of Healing* (New York: Harper and Row, 1965), p. 23.

[9]A. Worrall, p. 17.

[10]Agnes Sanford, *The Healing Light* (1947; rpt. St. Paul: Macalester Park Publishing Co., 1976), p. 6.

[11]A. Sanford, p. 8.

In the presence of a belief that good health is God's will for everyone and that the whole process is governed by strict laws, every failure carries the blame back to the suffering person. Guilt is added to pain.

This guilt opens the door to another way prayer functions in healing. If we confess our sins and receive forgiveness, we clear away some obstacles that prevent (or hinder) God's action in our lives. Our relationship with God is purified. We feel more deeply the presence of God and are able to function more effectively. Indirectly, this kind of prayer is related to good health—spiritual, mental, and physical. Steve Land defines it this way: "Our prayer for healing is a prayer to know this wounded, healing savior and to be in relationship with Him. To pray in the name is to pray in the presence is to pray in the will of Christ. And all prayer in the name shall be done."[12]

Discuss how physical illness might be related to spiritual illness, such as guilt.

Prayers for Healing

Francis MacNutt has a helpful practical analysis of prayer functioning to heal in his book *Healing*. In Part III he divides healing situations into four different kinds and gives directions for praying in each.

1. *Sickness of our Spirit*. This is caused by our own personal sin(s). The appropriate healing prayer is for forgiveness, with genuine contrition.

2. *Emotional sickness*. This is caused by the hurts we have felt because of the sins of others. Here the appropriate healing prayer is for inner healing (the "healing of memories," in Agnes Sanford's phrase). This is much more complex, and MacNutt recommends Mrs. Sanford's book,

---

[12]Brown, p. 4.

The Healing Gifts of the Spirit (Lippincott, 1966).

3. *Physical sickness*. This is caused by disease or accident. Here the appropriate prayer is a petition for physical healing.

4. *Sickness caused by demonic oppression*. The healing prayer is a prayer of deliverance, addressed to the oppressing demons rather than to God. It is more like a word of command (discussed more fully in this study in the chapter "The Role of the Word").[13]

The viewpoint that God (Christ, the Holy Spirit) is the real healer, either directly or through human agents, is presupposed behind the first three situations. The fourth is related to the psychic explanations of a healer's power to heal, discussed in this study in the sections on "The Role of the Healer" and "The Role of the Word."

In a later book, Francis MacNutt stresses healings that are not instantaneous but gradual. He has found more of this type than dramatic sudden healings. Because of this, he recommends practicing "soaking prayer."[14] A "soaking prayer" takes time and requires numerous repetitions (or treatments). It is not saying something all the time but continuing an initial prayer in song, tongues, or silence combined with the laying on of hands. Since hours may be involved, perhaps days as well, MacNutt sees "no reason why we can't pray for an hour and then take a ten minute coffee break before coming back to pray again."[15]

Discuss the values you see in the practice of "soaking prayer."

---

[13]MacNutt, pp. 146-148.

[14]MacNutt, *The Power to Heal* (Notre Dame, Indiana: Ave Maria Press, 1977), pp. 39-55.

[15]MacNutt, *Power*, p. 42.

6 The Role of the Word

Readings from Luke: 4:31-41; 5:7-26; 6:6-11; 7:1-10; 8:26-39, 40-56; 9:1-6; 9:37-43; 10:1-20; 13:10-13; 18:35-43

Speaking the right words was another important factor in the healings Jesus accomplished. "In his ministry, Jesus took the power of words with utmost seriousness."[1] Usually the words used for healing were in connection with casting out an "unclean spirit."

"Word" in this section of our study is used in the ordinary sense of a word (or words) spoken to another. It is not "the Word" of the prologue to the Gospel of John. That conveys a very different meaning. There "the Word" is a pre-existent creative power that became incarnate in Jesus of Nazareth.

How Jesus Used the Word

In the first healing story in Luke, the introduction to the story reports that "his word was with authority" (4:32). The phrase "with authority" is the usual translation of a Greek phrase that literally means "out of himself" or "out of his own being." The words Jesus used were not based on some earlier authority, but spoken out of his own authority. He did not usually quote Moses, for example, or the prophets as the authority for his words but took the full responsibility upon himself.

Neither did Jesus speak the healing word in "the name of" someone else, not even "in the name of Yahveh." He was himself the source of his power. This self-source,

---

[1] T. and S. Emswiler, p. 21.

45

however, was not because of his intrinsic divine powers according to Luke-Acts. It was the presence of the Holy Spirit within him that gave him this power. In Luke's phrase, "the power of the Lord was with him to heal" (5:17). (See also Acts 2:22 and 10:38.)

In this first story, Jesus cured the man with the unclean spirit by speaking the word of command: "'Be silent, and come out of him'" (4:34). Those who were present "were all amazed and said to one another, 'What is this word? For with authority and power he commands the unclean spirits, and they come out'" (4:36).

The pattern is the same in the stories that follow. The central theme is the power of Jesus' word to command and to be obeyed. The dynamics are those of spiritual power; the superior controls the inferior.

Immediately following the first story of healing is another one which implies the same dynamic. Jesus was in the home of Peter in Capernaum, and Peter's wife's mother was ill with a fever. Jesus "rebuked the fever, and it left her" (4:39). The fever was understood as something that, when "rebuked," would leave her.

The story of the paralyzed man who was let down through the roof (5:18-26) shows the authority of Jesus' word(s) in a different setting. Jesus pronounced forgiveness, demonstrating his authority to forgive sins. This healed the man's lameness. Both the healed man and the people (displaying the characteristic Jewish understanding of miracles) responded by glorifying God, who had acted in and through Jesus. Jesus used only words to heal the man with the withered hand (6:6-11), without any mention of unclean spirits or forgiveness of sins.

A striking example of the authority of Jesus' words is shown in the healing of the centurion's slave. The centurion's faith was so strong that he told Jesus it wouldn't be necessary to go to him personally: he said just "'say the word, and let my slave be healed.'" Jesus commended him, saying "'not even in Israel have I found such faith.'"

The story of "the man from the city [Gerasa] who had demons" (8:27) is a full-fledged story of possession and

46

exorcism (although the official term "exorcist" as one who casts out demons is never applied to Jesus in the New Testament). When Jesus asked the possessing demon his name (8:30), the answer was "Legion," probably referring to the number of soldiers in a Roman Legion. Luke explains that "many demons had entered him." At Jesus' command, they left him and entered a nearby herd of pigs, which rushed into the sea and perished.

Jesus restored a dying child with the words, "Child, arise" (8:54). He cured a particularly violent case of possession by rebuking the unclean spirit (9:42). Jesus used both words and laying on of hands to heal the bent over woman (13:12-13). He healed the blind beggar at Jericho by the words "Receive your sight," but added "your faith has made you well" (18:42).

All these stories teach the authority of Jesus' words, especially his authority over unclean spirits (or demons) possessing individual persons.

How the Disciples Used the Word

Jesus gave the twelve disciples "power and authority over all demons" (9:1). Later, he sent "seventy others" (10:1) out to prepare the way for his coming. They "returned with joy, saying 'Lord, even the demons are subject to us in your name'" (10:17). In Acts, the disciples continued to heal and to cast out demons, but now it was usually "in the name of Jesus." Paul, for instance, cast out the "spirit of divination" (Acts 16:16) that was possessing a slave girl with the words, "I charge you in the name of Jesus Christ to come out of her" (Acts 16:18).

From this beginning, the church throughout history has continued to recognize that "possession" by "a spirit," or "spirits," or "demons," or "devils" is a real phenomenon. Consequently, it has in its Roman Catholic and Orthodox forms, at least, developed rituals for exorcism and standards for becoming a qualified exorcist. In all of these, the principle has remained constant: it is the command of the exorcist, in words often formalized and addressed directly to the possessing spirit, that drives out the unwanted spirit. It is a struggle of spiritual power. The superior power of God-in-Christ (or the Holy Spirit, less commonly) forces the inferior spiritual power to obey.

Presupposed World-Views

Several possible "world-views" lie behind the whole notion of possession by a spirit and curing by exorcism. "World-view" is a somewhat clumsy expression to indicate the environment of human existence. It is a partial translation of the German word *Weltanschauung*.* English has no precise word for this. The French *milieu* comes close.

The world-view behind the New Testament accounts is that of apocalyptic Judaism. "Apocalyptic"* comes from the Greek word *apocalypsis,* which means "revelation" (hence the alternate titles The Apocalypse of John or The Revelation to John). This world-view believed human existence was best understood in the context of a great cosmic war between God and Satan (see Revelation 12:6-12). With Satan defeated in Heaven (see Luke 10:18 also), the earth was the place of the final stages of the great cosmic war. Satan and his "angels" (or demons as fallen angels) were busily plaguing the human race (see I Peter 5:8). One or more of these demons, or unclean spirits, could possess an individual person and must be "cast out" for him or her to be restored to health. This world-view is well-documented in the New Testament.

Another world-view lies behind the Gospel of John (which has no possession/exorcism healing stories), Colossians, and Ephesians. This is a Jewish-Gnostic* world-view, not directly related to this present study.

A still different world-view sometimes presupposed behind possession and exorcism comes from influences that see human existence in the context of Greek Orphic-Platonic thought. Possession and exorcisms were not related at all to the apocalyptic, demon-filled world of the great cosmic war but instead to the world of departed human spirits who occasionally possessed a human (or an animal!) and needed to be "cast out." This world-view is assumed by a Canon in the Church of England, John D. Pearce-Higgins, who is "possibly one of the most knowledgeable and successful exorcists."[2] Such an understanding defines humans as essentially spirits (spiritual entities) imprisoned in a physical body that is not really part of our essential being (which is purely spiritual). This viewpoint is sometimes combined with a belief in reincarnation, as in the Ze Arigo phenomenon (see pages 61-62). Sometimes it also is combined with or based on Gnostic presuppositions (as in Christian Science).

Are Demons Real?

But is all this true? A large percentage (but not all) of the well-educated, mainstream Christians are skeptical and tend to regard demon-possession as superstition. The outward phenomenon is real and requires explanations. We need to re-examine, the skeptics say, the older traditional explanation of possession by another spiritual entity. This skeptical attitude does not necessarily reflect skepticism about Christianity in general or the Bible in particular. It is often the attitude of devout and sincere Christians who are loyal both to their church and to the Scriptures.

How can Christians be skeptical when some Scriptures are so clear about the reality of demon-possession? We do not need to surrender the authority of the Bible when we raise questions about the reality of demons; we do need to reexamine the Bible's authority and to understand it in a new way.[3] Many issues in our Christian past and present have not been settled by biblical statements. Some parts of the Bible sanction slavery, polygamy and the inferiority of women in passages that are very clear. Consideration of all four commonly recognized resources for truth—Scripture,

---

[2]Martin Ebon, *The Devil's Bride. Exorcism: Past and Present* (New York: Harper and Row, 1974), p. 200.

[3]See, for example, D. Nineham, *The Use and Abuse of the Bible* (London: Macmillan, 1976).

> Do you believe that "spirits" of some kind actually possess persons? Is exorcism dealing with the real world? What action would you take if a friend of yours came to you feeling like she (he) was possessed by a demon?

reason, tradition, and experience—sometimes leads us to a conclusion contrary to views recorded in parts of the Bible. Almost everyone now acknowledges this with regard to slavery and polygamy; most of us would also take this position on the inferiority of women. Others would express doubts about this biblical view of demon-possession.

The Bible itself has other world-views besides this late-Jewish apocalyptic one. It does not present just one viewpoint. Most of the Old Testament and some of the New presupposes human existence in a Satan-free world, ruled over by God alone. "The earth is the Lord's, and the fullness thereof" is the theme-song of the old Hebrew world-view (Psalm 24:1). Is the earth controlled by God or by Satan? Is illness God's punishment or discipline, or is it Satan's affliction?

How do these skeptics explain the outward phenomena? By psychological theories. As early as 1921 major studies paved the way for this current skepticism.[4] To explain modern psychological theories is beyond the scope of this present study. In general, they all call attention to the reality of personality disintegration, alternating personalities, multiple personalities, and other schizoid patterns. They all see the cure in reintegration of personality into wholeness, unity, and health.

The celebrated case of the exorcism of Anneliese Michel is a clear expression of this modern skepticism. She died in Germany in the summer of 1976 after priestly exorcisms conducted secretly at her parents' request with the official permission of the bishop of Wurzburg Dr. Josef Stangl.

-----

[4]T. K. Oesterreich's classic *Possession and Exorcism Among Primitive Races, in Antiquity, in the Middle Ages, and in Modern Times* (New York: Causeway Books, 1974).

During months of efforts of exorcism, she was not given medical help.

Criminal negligence charges were filed against Anne-liese's parents and the two priestly exorcists. Clinical psychiatrists were called in as experts. Their testimony largely determined the outcome. The parents and priests were convicted of "negligent homicide." Not merely convicted by the court, they were also "put down, ridiculed, and condemned by public opinion because of their belief in possession." [5]

On the other hand, there are some well-educated mainstream Christians who continue to understand the outward phenomena in the traditional ways. The French Catholic neurologist Jean Lhermitte for example, wrote that:

> ...what ever skeptics, unbelievers and the ill-informed may think, demonopathic manifestations are not extinct.... Are we sure of the real existence of an "unclean spirit," an "evil spirit" who prowls around us seeking whom he may devour? There can be no Christian who does not give an affirmative answer to this question.[6]

Lhermitte goes on to remind us of Baudelaire's famous words, "the devil's greatest cunning is to make us think he does not exist."[7]

Lhermitte's classic study distinguishes between true and false possession, however. In it he suggests that most so-called cases of possession are actually psychological disorders needing medical attention.

A similar stance is found in "The Possession Problem" by Richard P. Woods. He notes the "general sense of supernatural bewilderment"[8] that has resulted from the resurgence of interest in charismatic, spiritualist, and

---

[5]Felicitas D. Goodman, *The Exorcism of Anneliese Michel* (New York: Doubleday and Company, 1981), p. xiv.

[6]Jean Lhermitte, *True and False Possession*. Trans. (New York: Hawthorn Books, 1963), pp. 7-8.

[7]Lhermitte, p. 9.

[8]Richard P. Woods, "The Possession Problem" in *Begone, Satan!* (Huntington, Indiana: Our Sunday Visitor, Inc. 1974), p. 70.

exorcist phenomena, especially since the wide distribution of the book *The Exorcist* and its film sequel. "The problem with *The Exorcist*," he commments, "is not that it is bad, but that it is convincing, at least to the unwary."[9] He says that "*The Exorcist* case is particularly serious... because of the effect both the book and the film are having on a growing number of impressionable people."[10] Woods observes:

> The current heyday of diabolism is reaping much more than money; it is harvesting, or at least catalyzing, a whirlwind of spiritual and psychological disorders of frequently tragic consequences. A truly pastoral problem is in the making.... It is, simply, the problem of personal evil experienced as demonic possession, coupled with a desire, if not a demand, for exorcism.[11]

Fundamentalists, of course, form another group of moderns who affirm the reality of possession. Many of them, however, limit their recognition to cases of New Testament times.

Goodman sees the whole difficulty as one that is compounded by many other factors, especially the attitude of mainstream church leaders—one of "benign neglect"—and the prevailing skepticism regarding the reality of demonic forces and spirit possession. Finally, however, Goodman leaves open the possibility of real cases of demonic possession, noting: "While it is groundless to affirm that all such people [those who claim to be possessed] are possessed by unclean spirits, I would not rule out the possibility that some are actually so afflicted."[12] He does regard such cases, however, as very rare.

Another Kind of Healing Word

As a factor in spiritual healing, the word is not limited to commands addressed to possessing spirits. It also functions in less dramatic ways. Words of empathy, or understand-

---

[9]Woods, p. 67.
[10]Woods, pp. 67-68.
[11]Woods, p. 68.
[12]Woods, p. 75.

ing, or acceptance, or affirmation, or of love certainly function in a healing manner. They minister to real needs. They encourage and stimulate good health in all of its forms.

The speaker of these good words does not need special healing powers or ordination. The healing word may be spoken by anyone; the basic requirement is simply concern for the other. It is a willingness to be used by the grace of God for the redemption of those around us. It is the chief (or a chief) trait of the redemptive community. We cannot save ourselves; we can participate in the salvation of others.

In Protestantism we believe that this unordained healing word is a function of the priesthood of all believers. It is the principal ministry of lay persons, perhaps even the principal ministry of the church.

Also, as Protestants, we understand the healing (saving) word in a more formal sense. The Bible is the Written Word to be applied to the current needs by the Spoken Word, the sermon. The Written Word and the Spoken Word are equally the Word of God. We all understand the way the Word of God (written and spoken) brings us to "salvation"; we seldom permit the word "salvation" to have its full meaning, including wholeness and health in all its forms, both individual and societal. So the sermon is a healing as well as a saving word.

In what ways can you hear the Spoken Word (the sermon, for instance) as "healing" as well as "saving"?

The role of the word is thus an important factor in total health. It takes its place alongside all the other factors without becoming the essential one. The whole complex of factors is too intertwined for any one factor to be the most important one.

7 The Role of the Healer

Readings from Luke: 5:17-26; 6:19; 8:39; 8:43-48; 9:1—10:20; 11:20; 13:13; 17:11-19

Jesus as Healer

The Gospels make it very clear that Jesus had special powers to heal. In this chapter, we will examine the role that the healer himself or herself plays in the healing event. How much of the healing, or what part of the healing, is directly due to the special powers of the healer?

We can, first of all, acknowledge the reality of the healer's power. When Jesus was on his way to the house of Jairus to heal his daughter, a woman in the crowd touched the garment Jesus was wearing and experienced an immediate healing. In Luke's account, Jesus declares the healing event by asking who touched him and witnessing that he felt power go out from him (Luke 8:46). In Mark's Gospel, it is the Evangelist who describes the event as a power-flow from Jesus to the woman (Mark 5:30). That ancient explanation is still current as well as several others we will examine later in this chapter. The event, however, clarifies the role of the healer in the process of restoring an ill person to health and wholeness.

The Jewish Viewpoint

Jesus, as a Palestinian Jew of the Roman Empire, understood his healing powers as a typical Palestinian Jew of that time would have understood them. His explanation, as reflected in Matthew and Luke, was that God was acting through him. This was also expressed as the Spirit of God acting through him (the Holy Spirit = the Spirit of God).

The Jews did not attribute a healer's powers to the healer himself or herself. The healer was merely a chosen instrument of God. It was God doing the healing, not the healer. One way this Jewish understanding is revealed in the healing stories in Luke is by the expressions of gratitude to God that usually follow a healing. When the paralyzed man who was let down through the roof was healed, he "went home, glorifying God" (5:25). When the Gerasene demoniac was healed, Jesus instructed him, "Return to your home, and declare how much God has done for you" (8:39). On another occasion Jesus affirmed that his ability to cast out demons was "by the finger of God" (11:20). When Jesus healed the bent over woman, her response was that "immediately... she praised God" (13:13). When Jesus healed the ten lepers and only one—a Samaritan—returned to thank Jesus, Jesus' response was "'Where are the nine? Was no one found to return and give praise to God except this foreigner?'" (17:17-18).

What was implied in all of these episodes was made explicit in Luke 5:17: "the power of the Lord was with him to heal." It was made even more explicit in the second volume of Luke's work the Acts of the Apostles, when Peter described Jesus as "a man attested to you by God with mighty works and wonders and signs which God did through him..." (Acts 2:22). In another speech, Peter described Jesus as one who "went about doing good and healing all that were oppressed by the devil, for God was with him" (Acts 10:38).

In Acts, Luke went on to credit the healings performed through the apostles to the power of the Risen Lord. For instance, when Peter healed the paralytic Aeneas, he said to him, "Aeneas, Jesus Christ heals you; rise and make your bed" (Acts 9:32-35). The apostles repeated most of the healings that Jesus performed, including raising the dead, but always within the context of humans being the instruments of divine power.

Most modern Christian healers would share this interpretation (self-understanding) with Jesus and the apostles.

Oskar Estebany, for instance, explains his healing powers by saying that he feels he is "a channel for the Spirit of Jesus the Christ."[1] Olga Worrall instructs the healer to urge the patient to "relax and feel the presence of the God power flowing into every part of his [or her] being."[2] She and her husband Ambrose confess, "We know that no power exists in and of ourselves; we are merely the channel, the vehicle, for a power that is not ours to command."[3] Agnes Sanford agrees. She has described the healing of her baby's abscessed ears by a young minister as "the life of God" flowing through him for the healing of the child.[4]

In many other cultural settings, healers often understand their powers in a way that is similar in principle to that of the Jews (and Christians), but their religion requires a different name for the divine power that is doing the healing.

The Greek Viewpoint

Among the Greeks there was a different *kind* of explanation. Believing as they did in gods and goddesses and believing that these divinities took human form on occasion, the Greeks tended to understand a healer as a divine being in human form. A person with supernatural powers, then, was a supernatural being.

Luke gave us a story about Paul and Barnabas that illustrates the typical Greek viewpoint about miracles of healing. At Lystra the two apostles healed a man crippled from birth. When the people saw this, they exclaimed, "'The gods have come down to us in the likeness of men!' Barnabas they called Zeus and Paul, because he was the chief speaker, they called Hermes" (Acts 14:11). In Greek mythology Hermes was the messenger, or herald, of the gods and goddesses; he spoke for them. That's why Paul, the chief speaker, was thought to be Hermes. (Hermes may

---

[1]Krieger, p. 6.
[2]O. Worrall, n.p.
[3]A. Worrall, p. 9.
[4]A. Sanford, p. 3.

be more familiar to some readers by his Latin name Mercury.)

In the two Gospels (Mark and John) that reflect a more Gentile (Greek, in this sense) background, Jesus' healing powers were regarded as indicators of divinity. This is especially evident in the Gospel of John. For John, Jesus was one with God (John 10:30) and was himself the source of his healing powers. The healing miracles of Jesus were signs of who he really was: their function was to promote belief. The characteristic reaction to the healings of Jesus in John's Gospel was not to praise God, as it was in Luke, but to believe in Jesus as the one "from above."

The New Testament itself, therefore, gives us two explanations of the power of the healer, both conditioned by the prevailing cultural backgrounds of the times. In the Jewish explanation, it is God working through the healer. In the Greek it is the healer's own power. Today we are not limited to these ancient explanations, but we are obligated to consider the reality of the healer's powers in the cultural setting of the twentieth century.

Of course, the healer's own understanding of his or her healing powers is important data. It does not, however, have the same authority as the data about the healer's power to heal. The healer's explanation is often no more than the product of the healer's cultural and personal background.

The Power in a Healer

What is the source of power in a healer then? The healer's own explanation differs with the individual, the culture, and the time. Scientists have also explored this question. MacLeod quotes a scientific, verifiable healing event reported by L. E. Eeman, who described the cure of a patient who had been contorted by the effects of pain from acute sciatica. The only instrument of healing was a copper wire held in the scientist's right hand and the patient's left hand. After a few minutes in the relaxation circuit, he began to feel circulation and warmth in the affected parts. His muscles began to relax spontaneously and progressively. Eeman described what happened next:

> Suddenly unbearable pain attacks him. He turns pale, sweats profusely and literally writhes in agony. Moved by his screams, I break the circuit and calm returns. I inform him that experience convinces me that, if he will but have the courage to face pain in the circuit until it stops of its own accord, he will be amply rewarded. He says, "All right, go on, I'll stand it." I close the circuit again and, almost at once, agony! A quarter of an hour, possibly more, and suddenly peace and relaxation. The patient rests and gradually recovers colour. His clothes are wet with perspiration. He rises, tests his limbs in various attitudes that have been impossible for weeks, finds no pain, and leaves the room almost straight. After half a dozen treatments in the circuit, this chronic sufferer from sciatica becomes a swimming enthusiast at the age of fifty.[5]

MacLeod concludes from this that 1) some force was present, 2) the healer was not deriving his power from any Christian belief, 3) "it was, nonetheless, divine healing," 4) it is similar to healings in a Christian setting, and 5) it does not always happen, either in Eeman's office or in a Christian healing service. This power therefore does not seem to be limited to people of faith:

> There seems to be a power in the world (it is sometimes apparent in the laying on of hands) which cannot be exclusively claimed for men [or women] of Faith. It is, none-the-less, extended to men [or women] of Faith at times. Some call it 'odic force.' ...Spiritual Healers, it seems, have this force to a marked degree....[6]

Ambrose Worrall had a similar opinion: "There is evidence that spiritual healing power is demonstrated through people of many religions, and through some who have no religious affiliations."[7] Nevertheless he also believed that the power to heal comes from "the Supreme spiritual power," whatever it is called and whether or not it is recognized.

---

[5]L.E. Eeman, *Co-operative Healing: The Curative Properties of Human Radiations,* as quoted in MacLeod, p. 7.

[6]MacLeod, p. 7.

[7]A. Worrall, p. 164.

Macleod points out that all Christians need to keep whatever contribution to healing they (we) have within the larger context of healing and not make exaggerated claims for it. "The Church is not the miraculous element in a natural world," MacLeod observes. "The Church is the interpreter of what is in any event a miraculous world."[8]

Do you think a person can be a healer and not be aware of her (or his) ability to heal?

Modern Research

While scientific inquiry in this area is still in its infancy, we have definitely broadened our knowledge about the role of the healer through experimentation. Scientists have discovered that Olga Worrall's skin temperature rises 13 to 15 degrees when she is in a state of healing. Other healers create a similar effect. For instance, one of the people who has experienced therepeutic touch reports feeling "deep heat... generated inside my body" when Dolores Krieger's hands were on her. Similarly, those touched by Oskar Estebany have often reported that they felt heat from his hands.

Scientists have also discovered that the hemoglobin level changes and the brain waves change in both the healer and the recipient during a healing session. This data was gathered during Krieger's carefully monitored experiments in 1978 at the Langley Porter Neuropsychiatric Institute at U.C.L.A.[9]

More data comes from Kirlian (*pronounced KEER-lee-an*) photography, a new kind of photography initially discovered in 1939 by the Russian electrician Semyon Davidovitch Kirlian. Ten years later, Kirlian, now joined by his wife, Valentina, had 14 patents and announced their new

---

[8]MacLeod, p. 8.
[9]Krieger, p. 9.

kind of photography to the scientific world.

In Kirlian photography the object to be photographed, together with photo paper, is placed between two electrodes. When the electricity is turned on briefly, an image is formed on the paper. No "camera" is used. The basic method is now refined and has developed into a special optical instrument that permits direct observation of the image that is produced (or exposed) by the electrodes.

What the Kirlians learned and have now documented photographically is that all living things—human, animal, plant—emit an active "energy pattern" that is not exactly identical with the physical reality of the living thing. This "energy pattern" may extend beyond the physical boundaries, may be expressed in many different colors, and may show a wide variety of effects.[10]

The Kirlians are convinced that living things have two "bodies"—the one we see (the physical body) and an "energy-body" that we don't ordinarily see. When a third of a leaf's "physical body" was cut off, for example, Kirlian photography showed an "energy-body" that was still whole.

When used to study healing by a non-medical healer, Kirlian photography of the healer's hands during a healing session shows a significant increase in the size and intensity of the "aura" surrounding the fingers. Both Olga Worrall's hands and Dolores Krieger's have exhibited this phenomenon.

Most of the studies either assume or theorize that there is some kind of "energy flow" from the healer to the patient. This explanation may have originated in ancient times from the feelings of the healer at the time of the healing. "Who touched me?" Jesus asked, "for I felt power go from me" (Luke 8:46). Ambrose Worrall witnessed that "a flow of healing force... comes often in... healing procedures from the solar plexus region of my body."[11] One of Krieger's

---

[10]The Kirlians learned to recognize a healthy organism or a sick one from their study of the color of its energy pattern. Prior to the appearance of any visible symptom, they could detect an oncoming illness.

[11]A. Worrall, p. 18.

patients reported, "'I can feel the energy flow she transmits to me.'"[12]

Dolores Krieger is one of many who have found an explanation in oriental cultures and their religions. Christians may, at first, reject such answers on principle, but, for instance, the Roman Catholic Church, in its Vatican II deliberations, did not condemn those of other religions who "look...for answers to those profound mysteries of the human condition."[13] Krieger studied the health practices of Yoga, Aruvedic medicine (Hindu), Tibetan medicine (Buddhist), and Chinese medicine. She learned that they teach that there is "a subsystem of energy which is called *prana* in Sanskrit...." She came to the belief that this best explains the "human energy transfer" that seems to take place in spiritual healing. *Prana* doesn't translate into Western vocabulary easily. It has to do with "the organizing factors that underlie what we call the life process." *Prana* is therefore what creates and sustains and heals life itself.[14]

Normally healthy persons have an excess of *prana*. Ill persons have a deficit. *Prana* can be transferred from a well person to a sick one. Hence the following model:

> Conceive of the healer as an individual whose health gives him access to an overabundance of *prana* and whose strong sense of commitment and intention to help ill people gives him or her a certain control over the projection of this vital energy. The act of healing, then, would entail the channeling of this energy flow by the healer for the well-being of the sick individual.[15]

This, of course, is a purely natural explanation. The healer's *prana* is the source of power.

A less "orthodox" explanation is the one illustrated by the famous healer of modern Brazil, Ze Arigo (Jose Pedro de Frietas), who was killed in an auto accident on January 11, 1971.[16] Although he hadn't gone beyond the third grade and had no specific medical training, he was a remarkable

---

[12]Krieger, p. 9.
[13]*Nostra Aetate*, Art. 2.
[14]Krieger, p. 13.
[15]Krieger, p. 13.

> Attributing healing power to one's God is clearly a religious option but would such attribution make the healing situation any different—or better—in the long run?

surgeon and healer with an international reputation. Ze Arigo was investigated by a team of medical doctors from the United States in 1968. The head of that team, Henry K. Puharich, came to regard Arigo as "the greatest healer in the world."[17] No other so-called "psychic surgeon" has been so carefully investigated and verified.

Arigo was a "Kardecist"—a follower of "Allen Kardec" (real name, Denizard Rivail). "Kardec" was a nineteenth century professor who believed in the reality of "spiritualism." For the Kardecists, this does not mean an organized religion, or denomination, nor does it encourage the more superstitious or ritualistic aspects of some spiritualists. They exemplify a sophisticated, intellectual type of spiritualism. Ze Arigo explained that his healing powers were due to a guiding spirit that actually did the healing. His guiding spirit was Adolpho Fritz, a German physician who had died in 1918. When Arigo was "possessed" by Fritz in a trance, he was the great healer. When he was not "possessed," he was a simple Brazilian peasant, loyal to his Catholic Church. He saw no contradiction in being Catholic and a Kardecist at the same time.

Many other healers have a similar understanding of their power to heal. One of the best known of these in the United States was the Baptist Sunday School teacher Edgar Cayce. Thomas Sugrue has written his story in *There Was a River*.

This explanation assumes the immortality of the soul and the actuality of reincarnation. It has many points in common with the understanding of what a human being is

---

[16]His story has been told in many places, most fully in *Arigo: Surgeon of the Rusty Knife*, by John G. Fuller (New York: Thomas Y. Crowell, 1974).
[17]Fuller, p. 210.

in the thought of Elisabeth Kubler-Ross and Dale Moody as they report experiences of those who reportedly die briefly and return to life.

This "possession" viewpoint brings us back to the Jewish-Christian understanding that the healer is an agent of another power working through him or her. For Oskar Estebany, Olga Worrall, Agnes Sanford, and Kathryn Kuhlman, the real power at work through them is God or Jesus Christ. For Ze Arigo it is Adolpho Fritz. The principle is the same. The active powers are different.

For George MacLeod and Dolores Krieger, the healer possesses some special force. He prefers the terminology of Baron von Reichenback and calls this force "odic power." She prefers the Hindu Sanskrit term *prana*.

> What difference does it make (if any) to regard the power at work in healing as Jesus Christ, or the Holy Spirit, or some other power?

Becoming a Healer

How does a healer get to be a healer? The apostle Paul believed it was a special gift of the Holy Spirit, or of God, or of Christ (see I Corinthians 12:4-7), and not for everyone (I Corinthians 12:27-30). A healer was a person with a special gift. Francis MacNutt says that it is precisely a divine gift and not a natural endowment that enables a healer. This gift is "resident in God—the Father, Son, and Holy Spirit. It is the Father, Jesus and the Spirit who heal. And they dwell within each Christian."[18] He believes that "every Christian, then, has the potential for healing," but "some people have a special gift of healing."[19]

---

[18]MacNutt, *Power*, p. 90.
[19]MacNutt, *Power*, p. 91.

Dolores Krieger recognizes that healers are persons with a special ability, but she believes that this special ability can be taught to anyone. In this, she follows the lead of her teacher Dora Kunz. Dora Kunz, however, was born with a unique sensitivity to subtle energies surrounding living things, according to Dolores Krieger.

Church leadership in general, both the clergy and the laypersons, is not currently given any training in what Olga Worrall calls "the Art of Healing." Both seminaries and lay schools are concerned about spiritual and mental illnesses, and both offer courses in "Pastoral Care and Counseling" for the healing of non-physical illnesses. But the extensions of this concern to physical illnesses have been surrendered to the medical profession. Mrs. Worrall laments that our pastors are not taught the art of healing in seminaries. She freely acknowledges that there are charlatans who are "pseudo-healers," doing more harm than good. If local churches would include well-trained legitimate healers on their paid staff, she says "there would be no need for the pseudo-healers."[20]

Discuss how a healer on your local church staff would be (or is) accepted. Would credentials be important? If so, what kind?

If you had a healer on your local church staff, what impact would that have on your church counselling ministry? (or if you have one, what impact has it had?)

The uncertainties about the teachable elements in healing make implementation difficult. We may have to learn to live with these uncertainties. Many, however, would agree with George MacLeod that "concern [or love] is the secret of healing."[21]

---

[20]Hopkins, p. 3.

[21]MacLeod, p. 3.

8 The Role of Malady

Readings from Luke 1:8-25, 57-66; 4:23-26; 5:17-27; 6:17-19; 8:26-39; 9:1, 37-43; 10:17-20; 11:14-26; 15:11-32; 21:5-28; 22:14-23, 31-32; 23:1-49

"Malady" is a very general word, not commonly used. Originally Latin, it passed into Old English from French. In each case, it means "sick." The term includes all kinds of sickness—disease, malnutrition, feebleness, fragmentation (unwholesomeness), disorderedness. It applies both to persons and to society and includes conditions that arise from all sources, even accidental injuries. Incorporating mental, spiritual and physical sickness, it commonly includes all kinds of pain and suffering—physical, mental, and/or spiritual. It is an umbrella-word, covering a large variety of things that are subjects for healing. This chapter asks about the role(s) that malady plays in human life—and especially in Christian human life.

The Universality of Malady

Malady is the common experience of all persons; no one is exempt. Disease germs and viruses and bacteria are no respecter of persons. Headaches, backaches, and footaches are part of the larger network of aches that humankind knows first hand.

Malady is not limited to the physical aspects of life: it afflicts the mental, emotional and spiritual dimensions also. Mental anguish, hurt emotions, and the pain of remorse and guilt are also common for all of us as frail human beings. There is no way to become mature without making mistakes that hurt us as well as others. It is profoundly true that "good judgment comes from experience, and experience comes from poor judgment." Pain and suffering are the price we all must pay for the progress we make in our earthly life. "Growing pains" may not apply to normal healthy physical growth, but no one can escape them in all the other aspects of life. Malady is a universal experience.

The Old Hebrew View of Malady

In most of the Bible, especially in the Hebrew scriptures (our Old Testament), all things have their source in God (Yahveh). Some of our malady is imposed on us by other humans in their use of the freedom granted by God, but this kind of malady is not a mystery. The maladies that have their origin beyond the human level—maladies such as storms, earthquakes, disease, famine, and birth defects—were all believed to come from God in the old Hebrew mentality. Yahveh alone was the source of all good and all evil, of both light and darkness (see Isaiah 45:7). Maladies from God even included those mediated by humans, such as wars and invasions. In this view, such divinely caused maladies were understood as punishment for disobedience or discipline to exercise our obedience.

Reflecting this viewpoint, Luke began his Gospel with an account of the priest Zechariah, who was struck dumb for a while as punishment for doubting the message of God given through the angel Gabriel (1:8-23, 57-66). The same understanding of malady is reflected in Luke 4:23-26, where Jesus reminded those in the synagogue at Nazareth of the famine God inflicted on the Israelites in the days of Elijah. It appears also in Luke 5:17-27 in the story of the paralyzed man whose friends lowered him through a hole in the roof. Jesus forgave his sins, the cause of his paralysis.

In this old Hebrew understanding, the cure for malady was repentance. If the trouble was God's punishment or discipline, then obedience and right living would end the malady.

Another Biblical View

In the centuries just preceding the coming of Jesus, the people of Israel underwent some profound changes. Temple sacrifices were reestablished after the return from Babylonian exile (in the sixth century, B.C.E.) and, with one or two interruptions, continued until the Temple was destroyed by the Romans in 70 C.E. Even though the Temple was still functioning, however, the center of religious life was shifting away from the Temple to the synagogue.

Survivors of the nation of Judah, in the period of the exile and afterward, came to be known as "Jews." Away from Jerusalem, they formed worship and study groups called "synagogues." The leader (or teacher) was the "Rabbi." The new form of religion was "Judaism."

The intellectual and religious center of Judaism was not Jerusalem; it was Babylon. A thousand years later, it was still Babylon. The guiding principles of fully developed Judaism were formulated by Babylonian Rabbis and were collected together in their classical form in the Babylonian Talmud (ca. 500 C.E.).

In this Babylonian setting, there was a religious and intellectual influence on the Jews that gradually persuaded them to think differently about the source and function of evil and malady. In this newer understanding, probably adapted from Babylonian and Persian religion, the origins of malady were not ascribed to God (Yahveh). Human existence was more easily understood if Yahveh had an "enemy" who caused all the maladies. This cosmic "enemy" had even rallied an army of spiritual forces to dislodge Yahveh as Ruler. "The Enemy" wanted to take over the universe. It was this "enemy" that caused all of our troubles.

The Hebrew word for "enemy" is *satan*. Soon the noun "enemy" (*satan*) became a name (Satan). The post-exilic Jews began to think that malady came from Satan and his "angels" (spiritual forces in his rebellious army). It's somewhat confusing to have two kinds of angels, so Jews increasingly began to call the bad angels (agents of Satan) "demons."

This "late Jewish" view (in contrast to the "old Hebrew" view) was well developed and popular in the Judaism of Jesus' time. Like the other, older view, it is also reflected in Luke. Most of chapter 21 is focused on the great cosmic battle between God and Satan. It describes briefly the troubles and tribulations that Satan is causing (and will cause) in these "last days" of the great cosmic war. Thus the famines, wars, earthquakes, pestilences, terrors, and persecutions (21:10-12) are not from God, but from Satan and his demons.

This view of malady lies behind all the stories in Luke about cures that are accomplished by casting out a demon or an unclean spirit. Luke reports, for example, that "those who were troubled with unclean spirits were cured" (6:18). The man in "the country of the Gerasenes" was possessed by "many demons"—a whole "Legion" of them (8:26-39). "The demons came out of the man and entered the swine..."(8:33). Another case of violent demon-possession is reported in 9:37-43.

Jesus gave his disciples "power and authority over all demons and to cure diseases" (9:1). Accordingly, Acts (the second part of Luke-Acts) records many instances of the disciples healing and casting out demons. In a report found only in Luke, Jesus appointed "seventy others" (10:1) to go ahead of him, two by two, and prepare the way for his visit. They "returned with joy, saying, 'Lord, even the demons are subject to us in your name'" (10:17). Jesus responded by saying "I saw Satan fall like lightning from heaven" (10:18), apparently referring to the belief that the cosmic war was over in heaven and that Satan's final fling was confined to earth.[1]

Among the disciples, Judas was "Satan-possessed" (22:3). Luke traced his betrayal to the Evil One. Satan tried to "get" Peter also, but Jesus intervened and saved him

---

[1]See Revelation 12:7-12 for a more detailed expression of this.

(22:31-32). All these passages make it clear that the source of malady was Satan, not God as in the "old Hebrew" view. The cure was not repentance; the cure was now exorcism.

Malady and Healing in Antiquity

In the Greek healing tradition, the centaur Cheiron, foster-parent of Asklepios, was wounded by one of Heracles' poisoned arrows. The wound was incurable but not mortal. Thus Cheiron became "the wounded healer." The wounded healer is more effective than the non-wounded one. His/her wound plays a positive role in healing others. The wound that will not heal is called the "Cheironian wound." It makes possible compassion (suffering with) and empathy.

A parallel to this tradition in Hebrew scriptures is found in the story of Jacob wrestling all night with his divine adversary. He emerged with a thigh that was put out of joint (Genesis 32:22-32). Then Jacob the Cheater became Israel. It was a changed person who healed the long standing alienation from Esau and became the father of the twelve tribes.

More to the point for Christians is the realization that our great Wounded Healer is Jesus. As Joseph Fichter reminds us, "...some Christians seem to have forgotten that the suffering of their savior was considered a necessary prelude to the joyful Resurrection."[2] Or, in the language of the Isaiah scroll that spoke so meaningfully to the early Christians, "he was wounded for our trangressions, he was bruised for our iniquities; upon him was the chastisement that made us whole, and with his stripes we are healed" (Isaiah 53:5).

Theologians have been occupied with the mystery of the atoning death of Jesus throughout Christian history. Their struggle to understand and rationalize our salvation experience continues. No "answer" is in sight. The mystery

---

[2]Fichter, p. 17.

may be permanent. It may be a perpetual reminder of our human limitations as we ponder the divine. But however we fail to see the whole, it is nevertheless true that Jesus is somehow our "Wounded Savior (Healer)."

A further example of the wounded healer, on the post-crucifixion discipleship level, can be seen in the Apostle Paul. He had some kind of "thorn... in the flesh." He regarded it, at first, as a handicap, "a messenger of Satan, to harass me," he wrote to the Corinthians (II Corinthians 12:7). He could not get rid of it. Like Cheiron's wound, it was not fatal, but it would not be cured: "Three times I besought the Lord about this, that it should leave me," he wrote (II Corinthians 12:8). But it didn't. Moreover, he came to realize that the thorn was not the handicap he thought it was but actually made his work more effective.

If the "thorn" made Paul's work more effective, was it really from Satan?

What the "thorn" was is now unknown and probably beyond recovery. For our purposes, it isn't even necessary to know. It was probably what he referred to in Galatians 4:13 as "a bodily ailment," a condition that made him a "trial" to them. Beyond this, we can only speculate. Whatever it was, it served finally to advance the good news of God's salvation in Jesus Christ.

Shamanism

The whole pattern of salvation—health—wholeness by means of a savior who has suffered, died, and risen again is one that has several parallels in primitive religions. We understand these as "foreshadowings" of the Christ-event. Both primitive religions and the Christian experience come from a common universal need of humans, well discussed in the closing chapters of *Reflections on the Psalms* by C.S. Lewis.

In certain primitive religions, there are universal elements that are still practiced and yet are modern survivals of very ancient, pre-Christian ideas and rituals. Most appropriate for our study is the role of the "shaman"—a kind of a combination of doctor and priest. In less accurate but more popular terminology, a "shaman" (male or female) is a "witch-doctor," or a "medicine man," with special powers.

The classic study of shamanism is the one by Mircea Eliade called *Shamanism: Archaic Techniques of Ecstasy*. Eliade, a professor at the University of Chicago, studied shamans in many primitive cultures and concluded that one common way a person became a shaman was through a special sense of being "called." This "call" is usually introduced by a "hysteroid crisis," an ecstatic experience of some kind believed by the tribe to be the result of intervention by "the spirits." The emerging shaman is taken by the spirits into the spirit-world and taught the secrets that give the shaman his or her powers.[3]

Prominent in the early stages of preparation is a serious illness:

> That such maladies nearly always appear in relation to the vocation of medicine men is not at all surprising. Like the sick man, the religious man is projected onto a vital plane that shows him the fundamental data of human existence, that is, solitude, danger, hostility of the surrounding world.[4]

Not only is the emerging shaman inflicted with a serious illness, he or she also recovers: "... the primitive magician, the medicine man or the shaman is not only a sick man; he is, above all, a sick man who has been cured, who has succeeded in curing himself."[5]

In these cases, we can easily see that malady itself is not automatically an evil but has positive values as well. Sometimes it is necessary or essential to the health and salvation of the tribal members, who depend upon the "magic" of the shaman—a kind of "wounded savior"—a

---

[3]*Shamanism* (Princeton: Princeton University Press, 1970), p. 17.
[4]Eliade, p. 27.
[5]Eliade, p. 27.

precursor of the Wounded Savior himself. The Epistle to the Hebrews says this about Jesus: "although he was a Son, he learned obedience through what he suffered; and being made perfect he became the source of eternal salvation..." (5:8-9). John Sanford, commenting about people in general, says "there is reason to believe that in some cases an illness is a necessary part of a person's development."[6]

Modern Views of Malady

The biblical views we have already discussed are still alive today. The old Hebrew view that malady is divine discipline or punishment still functions in many Christian lives. The later Jewish view that malady is the work of Satan is also still popular among some.

Many Christians today, however, following a more modern approach, develop the ancient insight that suffering can have positive values. Robert Leslie says: "The Christian faith affirms the possibility of the creative use of suffering.... Psychiatrist Viktor Frankl, for example, described the positive role of suffering. Suffering is a part of life, he asserted; to remove suffering is to remove some meaning from life. Life takes shape through suffering."[7]

Of course, to follow this kind of understanding completely would make the whole quest for health, wholeness, and salvation a mistake. To be able to use malady creatively is a great insight. But that does not mean that all pain and suffering is good, to be welcomed and encouraged. It is obvious that most of our maladies are undesirable, at the very least. We live between the two extremes, usually seeking the cure but sometimes using the malady for our own well-being.

Often a serious illness provides an unparalleled opportunity for self-inventory and readjusting priorities. "Illness is a low-tide experience that reveals all the debris usually

---

[6]J. Sanford, p. 32.
[7]Leslie, p. 20.

hidden by high water."[8] After recovery, one's life may be in better perspective and the former illness may be seen as a blessing. Malady may be an invitation to wholeness, a positive step toward becoming a whole person.

Everybody knows, of course, that pain itself serves a valuable function. Charles L. Swan, now a retired missionary and college professor, tells of his experience:

> It was from a wise old Mennonite doctor that I learned the meaning of *pain*, at least one of its many meanings. We were walking around the campus of his home for lepers—people suffering from Hansen's disease. It was in Central India in the days before antibiotics and the medical breakthrough on leprosy....
>
> At a cottage for four men... a simple iron brazier was glowing in the middle of the room.... the doctor explained that Hansen's disease... causes the patient to become unable to feel pain in the diseased area.
>
> A day or two before this patient had, unknowingly, placed his right leg against the red-hot brazier.... the hot iron burned the flesh deeply before he could be aware of the danger...
>
> "See!" said the doctor. "Pain alerts us to danger... thank God for pain."
>
> Further along the way I asked the doctor a question... "There are many dangerous and destructive things which are not straight-forward with their warnings. They do not cause pain immediately. In fact they are often 'silent killers.' Sometimes they masquerade as excitement and pleasure... what can we do about such dangers?"
>
> The good doctor knew.... "Fortunately," he said, "human beings can feel the pain of others. It is a sad sort of leprosy that makes us lose our ability to feel the pain of others."[9]

Joseph H. Fichter has made a special study of the relation of pain to religion. He observed, "Human experience does not satisfactorily explain the prevalence of human misery. People often turn to religion as they struggle with these problems."[10] The religious question is not the one about the

---

[8]Leslie, p. 17.

[9]Charles L. Swan, "The Meaning of Pain," *Michigan Christian Advocate* (May 6, 1982), p. 2.

[10]Fichter, p. 20.

source of pain; it is one about the meaning of pain beyond its primary function of alerting one to danger. What is the meaning of chronic pain, and what is the religious response to it and to malady in general? Fichter reports three responses:

1. Pain is a mystery without explanation.
2. Pain is a blessing from God,
3. Pain is not from God and needs to be eliminated.

The first is a surrender of the quest for meaning, the second is the old Hebrew view, and the third the modern version of the later Jewish view that ascribes malady to Satan.

The "New Age" Visions in Scripture

The Hebrew prophets were the severe social critics of their time. Seeing injustice all about them, they cried out in the name of Yahveh against the wickedness that violated the intentions of God. Part of their strategy was negative, proclaiming a coming doom as Yahveh's punishment. This actually happened. The nation was destroyed by the Assyrians and the Babylonians. The remnants of the once proud nation (the ten lost tribes of Israel) were deported all over the Assyrian Empire and lost to further history. The rest (the Judeans) were later exiled to Babylon.

The prophets then proclaimed a new emphasis—Yahveh's forgiveness and the coming restoration, a theme present in a minor way before this time. At times, this message was proclaimed so emphatically that the prophets were carried away with the idea and proclaimed a new golden age of universal peace. These utopian dreams reached their highest peak in the post-exilic oracles in the last part of the Isaiah scroll.

The sun shall be no more
   your light by day,
nor for brightness shall the moon
   give light to you by night;
but the LORD will be your everlasting light,

74

and your God will be your glory.
Your sun shall no more go down,
    nor your moon withdraw itself;
for the LORD will be your everlasting light,
    and your days of mourning shall be ended.
Your people shall be righteous
    they shall possess the land forever.... (Isaiah 60:19-21a)

And again,

I will rejoice in Jerusalem,
    and be glad in my people;
no more shall be heard in it the sound of weeping
    and the cry of distress.
No more shall there be in it
    an infant that lives but a few days,
or an old man who does not fill out his days
    for the child shall die a hundred years old.... (Isaiah 65:19-20)

The wolf and the lamb shall feed together
    The lion shall eat straw like the ox;
    and dust shall be the serpent's food.
They shall not hurt or destroy
    in all my holy mountain,
                                    says the LORD. (Isaiah 65:25)

These visions of a new age solved the problem of evil by
eliminating it and were naturally congenial with the new
ideas of the "Jews" (surviving Judeans) about God's victory
over Satan in the Great Cosmic War. The "Revelation-litera-
ture" (apocalyptic literature) that forms the backdrop of the
earliest period of Apostolic Christianity combined these
ideas of the new age to come with the new age that would
follow the end of the cosmic war. In the language familiar to
us from the teachings of Jesus, the new age is the coming
Kingdom of God.

This apocalyptic understanding presupposes that all
malady is the work of "the Enemy" (Satan) and denies any
positive values. In the last analysis, all malady is evil and
slated for elimination. The Book of Revelation, the best
biblical expression of these ideas, promises that God "will
wipe away every tear from their eyes, and death shall be no

more, neither shall there be mourning nor crying nor pain any more, for the former things have passed away" (21:4).

Even if we think about a coming new age that will eliminate all malady, we are presently living in the old age and need to keep our focus on our times. In our times, as we have seen, some malady is a positive value.

The Difficult Questions

The healing ministry, with its roots securely in the ministry of our Lord, cannot aim at the elimination of all malady in our age. Some of it is always needed as the price we pay for progress in maturation. But how much do we need? Who has too much and who has not enough?

When the healing ministry is actually under way, who gets healed and why? Is there any way to see which malady needs healing and which needs accepting?

Are there times when we need to induce malady (at least mental and spiritual malady) rather than always seek to "cure" it? It has been wisely said that the function of preaching is "to comfort the afflicted and to afflict the comfortable." Wellness and illness are so interwined, in our age at least, that they define each other. We all experience both. Is the church called on to keep them "balanced"?

Faith in the providence of God should not depend on our health. God can heal those who are sick and broken; then faith is easy. But when, despite our best efforts, we are asked to live with pain and malady, a deeper and harder faith becomes possible—the faith that accepts endurance, not healing, as a way of life and still praises God. Some of us are called to that kind of faith.

9 Technique or Grace?

Is the healing process governed by laws of health? If so, then, as we master these laws, doesn't that give us the power to control the results? Health matters would then be cleared of their "supernatural" elements and God would be in the picture only as the designer and sustainer of these laws of health.

The Natural Laws of Health

A major part of good health does seem to be under such laws. We are increasingly conscious of the importance of good nutrition, vitamins, and proper exercise for the enjoyment of good physical and emotional health. Certain causes have certain effects. Our expanding knowledge about these causes and their effects supports the hypothesis that all health matters are governed by laws that we already partly understand.

Some of the "spiritual healers" of our time agree with this. Lewis Maclachlan, for instance, uses an example of a car which breaks down:

> The driver of a car who finds that the engine will not start does not hastily assume that the laws of nature have been interrupted, or attribute the failure of his engine to some mysterious exception to the universal order. If he is wise he takes his car to a garage where it can be overhauled by experts who will discover the defect and put it right. So when our prayers are apparently unanswered we should make a persistent search for the cause within ourselves...[1]

Christian Scientists also believe that healing in all forms is a scientific matter. Robert Peel explains that "Healing... is the gradual replacing of false concepts in the human mind with

---

[1] Lewis Maclachlan, *How To Pray for Healing* (London: James Clark and Co., 1955).

the pre-existent spiritual realities as they exist in the divine Mind, the only true consciousness...."[2]

Olga Worrall of the New Life Clinic advises those who want to begin a healing service in their church: "It is very important to teach the people about the laws governing healing. Spiritual healing is a science and certain rules must be observed, such as positive thinking, replacing fear with faith, the importance of love, changing the inner man, etc."[3] But Olga Worrall also cautions that "no one can promise a healing." All we can do is to "hope that if every condition is met with, a healing may take place." She stresses that healings happen in God's time, not in human time.[4]

Her late husband Ambrose Worrall, an engineer employed in his retirement as a consultant to a major aerospace corporation, favored "the scientific approach to all phenomena." He said: "...The quest here as elsewhere should be an open-minded search for truth about the eternal and unchanging laws of God. I believe that most so-called 'miracles' are... only the working out of these immutable universal laws on a higher level of consciousness and being than we know."[5] In an even stronger statement, he asserted, "Everything in Nature is according to law. We live according to the laws of health or the laws of disease. It is impossible to break any of Nature's laws.... Spiritual healing is a natural phenomenon. It occurs strictly in accordance with natural laws."[6]

Agnes Sanford begins her well-known book *The Healing Light* with a chapter called "God Works Through Us," where she says: "God does nothing except by law. But He has provided enough power within His laws to do anything that is in accordance with His will. His will includes unlimited miracles. It is for us to learn His will, and to seek the simplicity and the beauty of the laws that set free His

---

[2]Peel, p. 12.

[3]O. Worrall, n.p.

[4]O. Worrall, n.p.

[5]A. Worrall, p. 17.

[6]A. Worrall, p. 164.

power.'"[7] Elsewhere, Ms. Sanford writes: "A wise engineer studies the laws of flowing water and builds his water system in accordance with those laws. A wise scientist studies the laws of nature and adapts his experiments to those laws. And a wise seeker after God had better study the laws of God and adapt his prayers to those laws."[8]

Lawrence W. Althouse (a recruit into the healing ministry of Olga Worrall) expresses this viewpoint quite strongly: "All the practitioners of spiritual healing that I know believe that it is a law-abiding phenomenon."[9]

It is interesting to note that both the Worralls and Lawrence Althouse, with their strong affirmation of laws that govern healing, use the "gift" concept in their book titles. It is also interesting to see devoutly religious and dedicated spiritual healers, like those quoted above, committed to an assumption about the universe that has been given up by the scientific community since Einstein. The Newtonian physics of strict "cause-and-effect," backed by the philosophy of Immanuel Kant, is now violated regularly at the atomic level, according to modern physicists. In an age when physicists are dealing with mysteries beyond "cause-and-effect," some religious healers (as well as other Christians) are still clinging to the rationalism of the world before Einstein. As physics teacher Harry W. Ellis has reminded us: "...the assumption that the universe operates according to rational principles... is not only unproven, but unprovable."[10]

Healing As the Gift of God

In contrast to those who regard health as strictly governed by universal laws, some healers, together with the mainstream of the church, have traditionally regarded healing as a divine gift. The healer Kathryn Kuhlman

---

[7]A. Sanford, p. 5.
[8]A. Sanford, p. 9.
[9]*Rediscovering the Gift of Healing*, p. 36.
[10]*Presbyterian Survey* (April 1982), p. 9.

assumed this point of view. Francis MacNutt says it this way: "There is no one method of technique that always produces results: God wants us to depend on him—not upon a technique."[11]

"Grace" is our English word for the Greek word *charis,* meaning "well-wishing." It stands for an intentional attitude of goodwill. It is from the same root as the Greek word *charisma,* meaning a "gift." Theologically, grace means God's freely given goodwill, a gift given unconditionally.

Traditionally we speak of being "saved by grace." *Soteria* (salvation), like *shalom,* is a large word that encompasses wholeness, peace, and good health. It is easy to understand why orthodox Christianity has traditionally regarded good health as a work of grace. This recognizes that God, not us, is in final control.

Although the controls are finally with God, that does not mean that we can disregard the causes and effects that we have learned about health. The "laws of health" are valid, as far as they go. But over and above our efforts and our careful observance of such laws, there is a greater power that we cannot control but only acknowledge.

We can now understand better why healings sometimes happen and sometimes do not. The failure of a healing to take place may not be due to violations of the laws of health or not meeting all the conditions but to factors included under the umbrella called "the grace of God."

The questions which come up at this point are similar to those universal questions that always get raised by the concept of salvation by grace. Theologically, does God desire the salvation of all? If we are saved by grace, then God either desires the salvation of all and does, in fact, save all (universalism) or God "elects" some to salvation but not others (predestination). We avoid these questions if we abandon the concept of salvation by grace and believe instead that God sets up the conditions of salvation, leaving humans free to choose and to enjoy or suffer the consequences of our choices.

---

[11]MacNutt, *Healing,* p. 195.

In matters of physical health, some spiritual healers clearly opt for salvation by obedience to the health laws, using similar logic (and, in the following example, similar caricatures of the other viewpoint). Commenting about "those parents and teachers who... taught us that God often willed us to suffer," Agnes Sanford says:

> If we think of God as a heavenly stage manager, jerking us about like puppets upon strings, this is a natural and indeed inevitable conclusion. God can do whatever He likes. We have asked him to make us well. He has not done so. Well, then, He must like us to be sick. In which case, if we are logical, we will not only stop praying for health but also stop taking medicine, for who are we to go against God's will?[12]

This kind of thinking drives her back into the rationalist-legalist position: "...The lack of success in healing is not due to God's will for us but to our own failure." It is due to "...a natural and understandable lack in ourselves."[13]

This type of thinking adds guilt to the ailment already present and even runs the risk of compounding the ailment. In contrast, Steve Land reminds us:

> All healing this side of the grave is temporary and partial.... We're in the process of being healed along with everyone and everything else in the world, and every once in a while God gives us a foretaste, a flash of what the end of history will be like. We call it a healing, and inevitably somebody starts trying to figure out how it happened.... But healing is not a cause and effect phenomenon....[14]

To understand spiritual healings as a work of grace rather than a result of some partially understood laws has several further implications. Most basic of all is the way our physical well-being is linked together with our well-being in spiritual and mental matters. All our "well-beings" are gifts of grace, essentially, even as we have traditionally acknowledged that our spiritual health is the result of God's grace.

---

[12]A. Sanford, p. 10.
[13]A. Sanford, pp. 11 and 8.
[14]Brown, p. 4.

What We Can Do

To assign health in general—all forms of health—to the grace of God is *not*, however, to remove the responsibility of doing what we need to do to promote and maintain good health. Our salvation by grace does not lead us away from good works but rather enables us to behave more righteously. The health we are given does not lead us away from health practices but rather enables us to do those very things that enhance the health we've been given.

The great heresy of every age in church history is the popular religious teaching that we determine our own spiritual health by the decisions and efforts we make. Reducing our spiritual life to such human dimensions blocks the greater power that is ours as a gift. It is the same with all other forms of health. To put ourselves in the driver's seat is to take over the role of God. That is the ultimate blasphemy.

The Two Graces

From the beginning of its history, the church has taught and practiced two graces with regard to illness. The earliest of these, stemming from the healings of Jesus, has been the grace that heals. George MacLeod, present leader of the famed Iona Community in Scotland, accurately notes that healing in the early church:

> was as normal as the Preaching of the Word.... This dual witness continued through the Medieval period.... This obedience dropped out from our Reformation witness.... Thus the healing of bodies, though, at first sight, it may seem an incursion into the present climate of our Church, is really normal. It is not an ecstatic Church that adopts it. Rather to neglect is to be subnormal.[15]

---

[15]MacLeod, p. 1.

It is obvious to every observer, however, that this healing grace has never been a panacea for all health problems. Jesus did not heal all the sick of his time, and the disciples did not end all sickness in theirs. In the constant experience of the church in history, it has continued to be "normal" that some are healed, more are not.

The Church therefore has taught and mediated another grace alongside the grace that heals. That second grace is the grace that sustains, or the grace that enables one to endure the illness or suffering or pain. In its preaching, the church has given much more emphasis to this grace of endurance than to the grace of healing, especially in mainline Protestantism. MacLeod said, in reference to healing:

> ...In so far as the Protestant witness has retained the practice, it has till recently become almost the prerogative of the sects: the Christian Scientist, the Spiritualists, the Pentecostalists, etc. In such hands, it is always in danger of becoming a heresy—that is, its over-emphasis upsets the balance of the full Gospel.[16]

What may be needed most, at this time in our Christian history, is a renewed recognition of the genuine tension that exists between the grace that heals and the grace that enables endurance. In that renewed recognition, there is some hope that the balance will again be restored. "There is a legitimate place for seeking physical, mental and spiritual healing as signs of God's activity, but there is also our belief that Christian life is a life of strength and courage in the midst of suffering...."[17]

An early example of this tension between the two graces occurs in the witness of the Apostle Paul. He prayed three times for the removal of his "thorn in the flesh," but God did not heal him. Instead he found strength to endure it, testifying that God's power was made perfect in his weakness (2 Corinthians 12:9).

---

[16]MacLeod, p. 2.
[17]Brown, p. 4.

Other Explanations for Healing

Medical doctors are aware that patients sometimes have recoveries from serious illnesses—even "terminal" ones like advanced cancer. In a religious setting, those with faith regard such recoveries as divine healing. But "miraculous" cures happen apart from religious settings and without faith in any supernatural activity. The uncertainty of healing, always present in spiritual healing circles, is also present in secular circles.

In secular settings, physicians call recoveries that medical science cannot account for "spontaneous remissions," or "spontaneous regressions." In 1959 surgeons T. C. Everson and W. H. Cole published a study of 112 of these cases, all they could establish since 1900.[18] In a more recent review of these unexplained cures, a team of doctors in Cleveland concluded: "We believe that no current theory offers an explanation."[19]

Sociologist David Hume gave another secular "answer" to healing uncertainties, substantially agreeing with secular medical opinion. He said:

> We hang in personal suspense between life and death, health and sickness, plenty and want, which are distributed amongst the human species by secret and unknown causes, whose operation is often unexpected, and always unaccountable."[20]

The philosophical theologian Paul Tillich identified one "ultimate concern question" as the problem of the maldistribution of pain and suffering. Within the bounds of human comprehension there is no answer. God is the "predominantly religious name" for the answer to ultimate questions.[21] Therefore, the mystery of the maldistribution of

[18]"Spontaneous Regression of Malignant Disease," *Journal of the American Medical Association*, vol. 169, p. 1758.

[19]George B. Rankin, M.D., Charles H. Brown, M.D., George Crile, Jr., M.D., "Spontaneous Regression of Hepatic Metastases from a Carcinoma of the Colon," *Annals of Surgery*, Vol 162, No. 1, pp. 156-169.

[20]Fichter, p. 19.

[21]Paul Tillich, *Christianity and the Encounter of the World Religions* (New York: Columbia, 1963), pp. 4-5.

pain and suffering is traditionally explained in Christianity by "the grace of God." In the same way, the mystery of healings and non-healings are questions of ultimate concern, answered in faith by "the grace of God."

What can we do about the "maldistribution of suffering and pain" among individuals? among the world's peoples?

This, of course, is not just an appeal to ignorance. If life's ultimate questions are not answered on the basis of the fundamental insights of our religious faith, the answers are both superficial and false.

From the larger wisdom of the main forms of the church in history, we have learned not to ask the ultimate question about salvation in "either/or" terms—"grace or works"— but in "both/and" terms. The grace of God and obedience to the laws of health, taken together, bring us closer to the ultimate mystery of total health.

10 Wholeness and Health

Readings from Luke: 4:16-21; 5:12-16, 17-26, 29-32; 6:6-11, 43-46; 7:21, 36-50; 8:43-48; 10:38-42; 11:34-36; 13:10-13; 15:1-22; 18:35-43; 19:1-10

Good health depends upon seeing the wholeness of persons, the wholeness of society, and the wholeness of God. Partial approaches are actually the sources of much sickness.

The Wholeness of Individuals

"In this new era of holistic medicine," declares Elisabeth Kubler-Ross, "we are finally beginning to appreciate that the human being is not only a physical body but consists of an intellectual, emotional, physical, and spiritual quadrant."[1] We only become whole and healthy as these four quadrants are brought into harmony.

Luke shows Jesus relating to persons in this total manner again and again. This included real concern for their physical wholeness. He restored walking to the lame (5:17-26), sight to the blind (7:21; 18:35-43), straightness to the bent over woman (13:10-13), clean skin to the leper (5:12-16), a useful hand to the man with the withered hand (6:6-11), and health to the woman with the flow of blood (8:43-48).

Although these are all important, Jesus was not concerned solely about physical problems. His activity in casting out demons showed an equal concern for the minds of people. After encountering Jesus, the Gerasene demoniac was "clothed in his right mind" (8:35). Jesus also showed

---

[1]Elliott M. Goldwag, ed., "Epilogue," *Inner Balance: The Power of Holistic Healing* (Englewood Cliffs: Prentice-Hall, 1979), p. 319.

great concern for emotional health. He calmed the fearful and taught the value and power of faith.

And Jesus felt equally concerned about the spiritual part of a whole person. He knew that one basic cause of spiritual sickness was sin and its consequences. Jesus declared that the sins of the lame man were forgiven, and his lameness was healed. When Jesus was criticized for fraternizing with sinners, his response was "those who are well have no need of a physician, but those who are sick; I have not come to call the righteous, but sinners to repentance" (5:31-32). The story of Jesus and "the woman of the city, who was a sinner" (7:37), is even more graphic in portraying the healing ministry of Jesus to spiritual sickness caused by sin. The three parables in chapter 15 illustrate further the theme of spiritual health through repentance. Another story, found only in Luke, makes the same point. "Salvation" came to Zacchaeus when he turned from his cheating ways; his spirit was healed.

In Jesus, as the black spiritual puts it, "there is a balm in Gilead." There is hope and healing for "the sin-sick soul." In spite of their sins, "Jesus affirmed persons and thus opened to them the way of wholeness."[2] In all these healings Jesus demonstrated his acceptance of the sinner. Jesus took persons where he found them. By affirming them, he gave them the inner freedom to repent and move toward spiritual health. We can see an example of this in the famous Mary and Martha story (10:38-42). When Martha rebuked Mary for not helping in the meal preparation, Jesus gently affirmed Mary. Perhaps what Mary was doing met a deeper need in Jesus than what Martha was doing. One can only wish that the story included Jesus' affirmation of Martha as well.

Sometimes spiritual illness is not the product of sin but an emptiness—an awareness of a lack of something. Jesus maintained his own spiritual health by frequently communing with God. Luke stressed the prayer life of Jesus and

---

[2]Narka Ryan and Catherine Elkiss, *Luke: A Search for Wholeness: Leader's Guide* (St. Louis, MO: Christian Board of Publication, 1979), p. 19.

noted carefully the times when Jesus left the people for a period of prayer (5:15; 6:12, etc.).

Jesus' God-consciousness was so real and effective that he may never have experienced this personal "emptiness" we sometimes feel. On the other hand, if he was fully human, he did. Gerald Jampolsky and Patricia Taylor have observed:

> Many of us are finding that, even after obtaining all the things one thought one wanted in terms of job, home, family, and money, there still seems to be an emptiness inside. Mother Teresa from Calcutta, India, calls this phenomenon "spiritual deprivation," and more and more people seem to be becoming aware of this phenomenon.... There seems to be a growing recognition of a need to feel a sense of fulfillment within rather than to experience success from without.[3]

The "sense of fulfillment within" might be expressed better as "an inner sense of affirmation and acceptance by God," for this inner need is not one we can meet out of our own resources.

The psychiatrist Viktor Frankl saw clearly the interrelatedness of all the human components. He called the spiritual dimension of a total person the *noetic* dimension, alongside the *somatic* (bodily) and the *psychic* (the mental). He regarded the *noetic* as the area "most characteristic of the human being."[4] Health was not the absence of sickness but "a positive and dynamic striving for wholeness."[5]

Fragmentation is an excellent term to express the lack of coordination between the human "quadrants" or "dimensions." "Inner unity" is a fine expression for good health. William James, the psychological pioneer at Harvard, defined religious conversion as the change in a person from inner fragmentation to inner unity. Much of contemporary "therapy" is a striving for this inner unity and peace. It is therefore very interesting (and important) to recall the ancient meanings of this Greek word *therapy*: it means both

---

[3]Goldwag, p. 145.
[4]Leslie, p. 16.
[5]Leslie, p. 17.

medical treatment and divine worship.

Personal integration requires a *center* around which all else is integrated. The new term "centering" attempts to express this integration of all human aspects around a central core. Religion is the only center that satisfies all the complications of a total person. To be "centered" on God is to be unified, whole, healthy and holy. As expressed by Paul Tillich, "Religion is the state of being grasped by an ultimate concern, a concern which qualifies all other concerns as preliminary and which itself contains the answer to the questions of the meaning of our life."[6]

But how does a person become *whole*? John Sanford reminds us that the way "is impossible to summarize" because each person is individual. Nevertheless he does say that:

> To become whole we must be involved with life. This earthly existence appears to be a crucible in which the forging of the whole person is to take place. Our life must have a story to it if we are to become whole, and that means we must come up against something; otherwise a story can't take place.... If we stand on the sidelines of life, wholeness cannot emerge.[7]

The psychiatrist Carl Jung called this movement toward wholeness "individuation." He regarded "individuation" as the source of all true health, according to John Sanford.[8] It is a process that moves toward wholeness but never gets completed in this life.

How do we move toward wholeness? The classical answer from the wisdom of the church is that we don't do it; it is a work of grace—a gift of God. We can take some steps toward wholeness: we can face our problems honestly, confess our inability to handle them by ourselves, be open to real communication, and keep ourselves in the means of grace. And, we can be cautious about accepting any

---

[6]Tillich, p. 4.
[7]J. Sanford, p. 19.
[8]J. Sanford, p. 15.

"do-it-yourself" program for wholeness and health. We can do a lot, but, most of all, we need the grace of God.

The Wholeness of Society

We are all aware of the tragic "brokenness" in the social patterns of the world today, with wars, famines, and political tyrannies. Economic opportunities are uneven and unjust. Ethnic prejudices run rampant. Women face discrimination everywhere. Children, as well as the aged, are often abused and neglected. We need the healing presence of Jesus Christ in the problems of societal wholeness just as much as we need his powers in our personal struggles for wholeness.

Luke, more than any other Evangelist, was aware of this aspect of the Gospel. In the very beginning of the story, the angel told Zechariah about John the Baptist. He would turn the hearts of the disobedient to the wisdom of the just and "make ready for the Lord a people prepared" (1:17). In "the Magnificat" of Mary, the mother of Jesus, a vision of the intentions of God included scattering the proud, putting the mighty off their thrones, exalting the lower classes, feeding the hungry, and sending the rich away empty (1:51-53). Later, when Jesus read from Isaiah in the synagogue at Nazareth he selected the passage that defined his full mission as including "release for the captives" and the freeing of those who are oppressed (4:18).

In our time, it is not difficult to find captives that should be freed or oppressed peoples that need to be rescued. For centuries, oppression has been a way of life for minorities and for women. Today we can see more clearly that this is a priority for the Gospel. Society needs healing and wholeness fully as much as the individuals in society. The message of salvation is for persons (individual evangelism) and for societal structures (the "social gospel"); it is not for persons only, or for society only, but for both.

Jesus demonstrated a real concern for the hungry. The beatitude in Luke is not spiritualized as it is in Matthew. In Luke we have the blunt promise "Blessed are you that hunger now, for you shall be satisfied," and the parallel warning "Woe to you that are full now for you shall hunger" (6:25). The ministry of Jesus included the feeding of the multitudes (9:10-17). The problem of the world's hungry has grown to gigantic proportions. We Christians of the "first world" are now the ones that are full; people of the "second" and "third worlds," especially those of the "third world," are the hungry. Furthermore, as "first-world Christians," heavily invested in capitalistic enterprises, industry and multinational corporations, we have contributed to the problem. Now it is imperative that we Christians recognize our involvement in the problem and take positive action to contribute to the solution.

Part of the sickness of society is exposed in the injustices of our economic system. Jesus warned about the perils of wealth and had some kind words for the blessings of poverty. Choosing a beggar's life for himself, he was careful not to get involved in a mad possession of "things" that characterizes "first world" economy. The beatitude about this theme is also much more direct in Luke than in its spiritualized version in Matthew. "Blessed are you poor, for yours is the kingdom of God," paralleled by "Woe to you that are rich, for you have received your consolation" (6:24).

On one occasion, when Jesus was asked to settle a family quarrel over the inheritance of property, he refused to interfere. He gave this warning: "Take heed, and beware of all covetousness; for a man's life does not consist in the abundance of his possessions" (12:15). Then he told his famous parable, perhaps best preserved in the newly discovered Gospel of Thomas, about the man who built larger barns to store his goods, only to die without enjoying them. An even stronger word of Jesus is expressed in his blunt instruction (given in a context now lost), "Sell your possessions, and give alms; provide yourselves with purses that do not grow old, with a treasure in the heavens that does not fail.... For where your treasure is, there will your heart be also" (12:33-34).

Only in Luke is the difficult parable about the dishonest steward (16:1-8). It is followed by several explanations

(16:9-13) which may be from the early church. Among these is an awareness of the perils of riches, "unrighteous mammon," in contrast to "the true riches" (16:11). The conclusion at the end is typical of Jesus' attitude: "You cannot serve God and mammon" (16:13).

Only Luke has the well-known story of the "ruler" who was "very rich" which illustrates again the concern of Jesus (18:18-30). The disciples were instructed in the radicalness of Jesus' prohibition of earthly treasures and reassured that their sacrifices were nothing in comparison with the benefits ahead. In Luke only is the well-known story of the widow whose tiny contribution outweighed all the huge ones, because it was all she had (Luke 21:1-4).

Jesus gave us no sociological analysis of societal sickness. He probably would have explained it as "demonic." He did have a keen awareness of the problems of wealth and poverty and offered appropriate warnings about the selfishness of the rich and the ongoing needs of the poor.

Modern studies have demonstrated beyond any doubt what we knew anyway by partial observations:

> Poverty and poor health go together. ...The black segment of the population (in the U.S.) suffers most.... If the medical care is surrounded by inconveniences and reinforced by long waits and impersonal treatment.... For the poor, a visit for medical care is frustrating, humiliating, inconvenient, associated only with emergency and pain.[9]

Add to that the nutritional factors in poverty, and it is easy to see why individual sickness is augmented by societal sickness and why wholeness and health for both go hand in hand. MacLeod warns us that:

> ...It is near blasphemy to pray for [Margaret who has tuberculosis] individually when there is a known cause [damp rooms in slums of Glasgow] which we should be tackling at the same time. Just as it is near blasphemy merely to pray that Jean, Mary, and John should be released from a fear neurosis—due to the present atmosphere of war preparation—without concerning ourselves about the international issues that make for war.[10]

[9]Leslie, pp. 137-139.
[10]MacLeod, p. 10.

Another societal illness that the Gospel challenges and promises to heal is the tragic plight of women the world over. In a culture that was notoriously sexist, Jesus was bold enough to include women in his disciple-group. In Luke, a short section (8:1-3) informs us about some of the women in the group, and adds that "they provided for them out of their means." This brief statement makes it easier to understand the presence of the women at the crucifixion and the crucial role they played at the empty tomb.

Luke paid more attention to women than did the other Gospel. What little we do have in the Gospels about the role of women has probably survived from a larger body of information.

On a more subtle level, Luke arranged the materials of his story in a special way which revealed his concern for women. Events and parables about men were sometimes "paired" with another event or parable about women. Elizabeth and Zechariah were "paired" with Mary and Joseph. Simeon is "paired" with Anna (2:25-38). Jesus healed a demon-possessed man (4:31-37) and then healed Peter's mother-in-law (4:38-39). Jesus healed a centurion's slave (7:1-10) and then raised up the widow's son (7:11-17). Insights about John the Baptizer (7:24-35) were followed immediately by insights from the attentions of the sinful woman (7:36-50). The Gerasene demoniac (8:26-39) was "paired" with the healing of Jairus' daughter and the woman with the flow of blood (8:40-56). The Good Samaritan parable (10:25-37) was "paired" with the Mary-Martha incident (10:38-42). Sandwiched between the parable of the lost sheep and the Prodigal Son was the woman with the lost coin. While the pairing cannot be seen as a rigid structure, it does reveal an unusual concern on the part of Luke to "give equal time" to women in the story.

So, in addition to Jesus, Luke may also have contributed to the healing of society's sexual brokenness through the perspective he chose to use in his Gospel. Although both contributed to the solution to society's injustice to women, they did not provide our final answer. What they did do was to point out the direction we need to take.

Our newly advanced sensitivity to the rights of women has a long way to go before we reach the desired end, but the direction is clear from the example of our Lord and the emphasis of Luke: we must follow it. Again, wholeness of women in society requires the wholeness of society itself. The healing of the person is impossible without the healing of the system.

What We Can Do

In United Methodist circles, all Christians are ministers, a few of whom are called to be pastors. Every Christian is called to ministry. What is ministry? It is the mediation of salvation. What is salvation? It is *shalom*, peace, wholeness, health. It is more than a spiritual condition. It is a total condition, involving all of us—body, mind, emotions, and spirit.

In our common call to minister, Jesus is our model. From the wholeness of his ministry, we get our vision of a holistic ministry. This vision calls us into healing the isolation and brokenness of individuals. Whatever the brokenness is, whether physical, mental, emotional, or spiritual, it is the object of our ministry. We participate in a redemptive community, and the grace of God works through us for others and through others for us. We can participate in that redemptive community.

But ministry to individual brokenness is not the whole mission. We are called to minister to the brokenness of society also. Individual wholeness and societal wholeness are intimately related. Our ministry calls us to oppose the social systems that permit, or even cause, hunger, poverty, racism, sexism, agism, and all the other signs of societal brokenness. This means active involvement in "worldly affairs" such as politics and economics and power struggles. Real involvement may mean the path of the cross.

Salvation—wholeness and total health—may be, in the last analysis, a free gift of God, a work of grace. It must be recognized, however, that salvation is not "cheap grace" but a call to costly discipleship.

11 New Testament Views of Healing

The earlier chapters took their starting point from the healing stories in the Gospel of Luke. This chapter enlarges the field to consider physical illnesses and their healing throughout the New Testament.

Illness is usually described in very general terms. In most cases anything like a modern diagnosis is impossible. Even when the illness is given a technical name—which is rare— it is an ancient diagnosis and not necessarily reliable.

The New Testament writers report only three technical diagnostic names: epilepsy (Matt. 17:15), leprosy, and dropsy (Luke 14:4). In each case the diagnosis is open to question. They identify two causes of illness and disease, and leave another cause unidentified.

Illness as Divine Punishment

The traditional Jewish view was that God sends illness or disease as punishment for sin (disobedience). The New Testament preserves this tradition, even as it modifies it. (Review "The Old Hebrew View of Malady" in Chapter 8.)

This view lies behind the story of the paralytic who was lowered into Jesus' presence through a hole in the roof (Mark 2:1-12; Matt. 9:1-8; Luke 5:17-26). Jesus' healing accompanied a pronouncement that his sins (unspecified) were forgiven. There is a similar viewpoint in the Gospel of John's story of the man who had been ill for 38 years waiting by the pool Bethzatha. After Jesus healed him, Jesus encountered him in the Temple and exclaimed, "See, you are well! Sin no more that nothing worse befall you" (John 5:14). Paul warned the Corinthians that it was because of their improper (sinful?) abuse of the Lord's Supper that "many of you are weak and ill, and some have died" (1 Cor. 11:30). In the Epistle of James, "confessing your sins to one another" (5:16) seems to be one element in the healing of the sick.

Paul's cursing of Elymas Bar-Jesus is a particularly dramatic instance of temporary blindness being the consequence of sin (Acts 13:6-11). The power to render blind was not Paul's, but that of the Holy Spirit working through Paul. When Elymas opposed Paul, he was exposed as a "son of the devil" and "an enemy of all righteousness, full of all deceit and villainy." His punishment was that he would be "blind and unable to see the sun for a while." Then "immediately mist and darkness fell upon him and he went about seeking people to lead him by the hand."

A similar punishment scene reported earlier in Acts was more severe. Because a man named Ananias and his wife Sapphira lied about the money they had from selling a piece of property, both died, and "great fear came upon the whole church" (5:1-11).

In addition to these examples, Luke's Gospel begins with the story of the priest Zechariah, whose disbelief of Gabriel's annunciation was punished by temporary loss of speech (1:20).

In accord with long established Jewish belief, when malady or sickness was understood as punishment for sin, the only cure was to repent and turn to a life of obedience. Of course, if death was the punishment, there was no cure.

Modifying this viewpoint, the New Testament also records Jesus as critical of it. One instance involves fatal calamity rather than illness or disease, but the principle is probably transferable. Those slain by Pilate's soldiers, or those killed in the collapse of the Tower of Siloam, were not being singled out for punishment because of their sins (Luke 13:1-5). This particular teaching, however, is probably directed at the larger question of reward and punishment in eternity rather than the consequences of sin in this life.

In one other story Jesus seems, at first, to be opposing the traditional view. In the story of the man born blind in John 9, Jesus is asked by his disciples, "who sinned, this man or his parents, that he was born blind?" The question is an odd one, because it includes in the list of suspected sinners the man himself. If he were born blind, and his own sin was the cause of his being born blind, then his sin would have to have been prenatal sin! Jesus' answer was a denial that sin was the cause: "It was not that this man sinned, or his parents, but that the works of God might be made manifest in him" (John 9:3). Here again, however, the story is not really concerned with our problem. The man was born blind so that Jesus could open his eyes, and the Evangelist makes the event the occasion for teaching that Jesus came into the world "that those who do not see may see" (9:39).

Illness as the Work of Satan

Much more common in the New Testament is the view that illness and disease are the work of Satan and his demonic helpers. (Review "Another Biblical View" in Chapter 8.) In most of these instances, the background is a different, and more recently adopted, cosmology than the more ancient one behind the divine punishment viewpoint. This newer cosmology presupposes that a great cosmic struggle is going on between a spiritually good power, God, and an enemy power, Satan. The Revelation to John describes the situation succinctly:

> Now war arose in heaven, Michael and his angels fighting against the dragon; and the dragon and his angels fought, but they were defeated and there was no longer any place for them in heaven. And the great dragon was thrown down, that ancient serpent, who is called the Devil and Satan, the deceiver of the whole world—he was thrown down to the earth, and his angels were thrown down with him. [A voice then warned:] "Woe to you, O earth and sea, for the devil has come down to you in great wrath, because he knows that his time is short" (Rev. 12:7-10, 12).

Luke's Gospel preserves a saying of Jesus that seems to reflect this same understanding of the current state of the cosmic struggle. "I saw Satan fall like lightning from heaven" (10:18).

This understanding of the environment of human existence was popular among Jews of the New Testament era, and consequently among the early Jewish Christians. It provided an explanation for illness and disease that no longer made God responsible for them. Instead, it was Satan and his angels (demons, evil spirits) that were the cause. They were exercising their wrath in their doomed struggle against the rule of God.

With this understanding, some of the illnesses and diseases, including deformities and birth defects, were thought to be due to demon-possession. The cure was obvious: to exorcise the demon. The first three Gospels report many such cases. The casting out of demons is a principal activity of Jesus in these Gospels. This is exorcism (although the Gospel writers never use the term), and it is done by a commanding word. The demon is verbally ordered out by a superior spiritual power, Jesus. (Review Chapter 6.)

Two of the Gospels, Matthew and Luke, seem to reserve the power to cast out demons for God alone. When Jesus does it, he is acting as God's instrument, rather than as a divine being using his own powers. In a summary of the story of Jesus in a later speech, Peter described Jesus as one anointed with the Holy Spirit and with power, and as going about doing good "and healing all that were oppressed by the devil, for God was with him" (Acts 10:38). In an earlier speech, Peter is reported as saying to the Jews that Jesus was "a man attested to you by God with mighty works and wonders and signs which God did through him in your midst" (2:22). These descriptions probably give us our best clues for understanding the powers of Jesus in the Gospel of Luke.

One saying of Jesus found in Luke is in the context of an accusation that Jesus was casting out demons by the power of "Beelzebul" (probably used as a synonym for Satan). His response was that it was not by Beelzebul that he was doing this, but "by the finger of God" (11:20). The statements in Acts help us to regard this as saying that it was God working through Jesus that effected the exorcism. The author of the Gospel confirms this by characteristically praising God when Jesus does "signs and wonders" (Luke 5:25; 8:39; 9:43; 13:13; 17:18; 18:43).

In the Gospel of Mark, however, Jesus seems to be casting out the demons by his own divine power. The demons are subject to him and recognize his divinity as a superior spiritual power. Jesus forbids the demons to reveal his divinity. The humans in the story, including the disciples themselves, never recognize Jesus as a divine being. Only after his death does a Gentile perceive his divinity, namely the Roman centurion at the foot of the cross (Mark 15:39).

In the Fourth Gospel Jesus is also perceived as a divine being on earth, but in this Gospel he never casts out any demons, probably because the Evangelist has a different world-view and no longer regards sickness as the work of Satan and his demons.

In the first three Gospels there is a certain freedom and flexibility in describing these supernatural causes of illness and disease. Demons and evil spirits seem interchangeable terms and both are subordinates of Satan. With this understanding exorcism is the only cure.

The means of exorcism is usually the word of command. But other means are casually mentioned. When Jesus came down from the Mount of Transfiguration, he was confronted with a boy possessed by an evil spirit. The disciples had been unable to cast it out. Jesus cast it out and then explained to the disciples that "this kind cannot be driven out by anything but prayer" (Mark 9:29). But this story has variations in the other traditions (see Matthew 17:20-21 and Luke 9:41-43). The story in Mark doesn't report any prayer in the exorcism, despite the concluding explanation. Instead, the active element is an implied faith on the part of the father (Mark 9:23-24). A manuscript variant in Mark 9:29 adds "fasting" as the necessary treatment, but fasting is not mentioned in the story either. Mark's account calls the possessing force "a dumb spirit" that the boy has had since childhood (9:17), and then "a dumb and deaf" spirit (9:25). Matthew's parallel account describes the boy as an "epileptic" (17:15), and also as possessed by a "demon" (17:18). Matthew attributes the failure of the disciples to their lack of faith, not to prayer or fasting. In Luke's account, it is "an unclean spirit" also called "a demon" (9:42), and the whole exorcism event prompts the observers to credit the healing to "the majesty of God" (9:43).

Sometimes the commanding and exorcising word of Jesus was effective at some distance from the possessed one, such as the healing of the Greek woman's daughter (Mark 7:24-30).

In the New Testament the power of the apostles to cast out demons derives from Jesus. Mark and Matthew both report that Jesus "gave them authority over unclean spirits" (Mark 6:7, Matt. 10:1). Luke reports that Jesus gave them "power and authority over all demons" (9:1). When returning from a mission and reporting to Jesus, "the seventy" that Jesus had sent out on a preparatory mission came back rejoicing, saying, "Lord, even the demons are subject to us in your name" (Luke 10:17). The ongoing power to exorcise demons was carried out in the name of Jesus. In the longer ending of Mark the Risen Jesus says of those who believe, "in my name they will cast out demons" (16:17). In agreement with this, the apostles in Acts use the name of Jesus to cast out demons. Thus Paul, when annoyed to the edge of his tolerance by a "slave girl who had a spirit of divination" that "brought her owners much gain by soothsaying" (Acts 16:16), spoke to the spirit that possessed the girl and said, "I charge you in the name of Jesus Christ to come out of her." The account reports that it "came out that very hour" (16:18). Using the name of Jesus to exorcise demons or evil spirits has continued in the church to the present time.

Unidentified Causes

New Testament authors did not regard all sickness as demon-caused. This is evident in the lists that distinguish demon-possession from other illnesses. In Matthew, for example, Jesus gave his twelve disciples "authority over unclean spirits, to cast them out, and to heal every disease and infirmity" (10:1). Then he instructed them to "heal the sick, raise the dead, cleanse lepers, cast out demons" (10:8). In Mark, it was reported that "they cast out many demons, and anointed with oil many that were sick and healed them" (6:13). Luke reports that Jesus not only gave them power over all demons but also power "to cure diseases" (9:1). In Acts Peter healed "the sick and those afflicted with demons" (5:16). In all these instances, it is clear that not all illnesses were regarded as caused by demon-possession. The other cause or causes, however, are not mentioned.

The healing of the non-demonic illnesses was usually regarded as by special divine power. In the thought of the Jewish branch of the New Testament Church, this power came from God through a healing agent—a person. Even Jesus was the human agent of God in the Jewish Christian church. The Gentile branch of the Church usually regarded Jesus as having divine power in himself. After Jesus' death and resurrection, this power continued by the use of his name. All this, whether Jewish or Gentile, parallels the Asklepian tradition in Greek medicine. Its healing centers and sanctuaries were the hospitals of the Hellenistic world. (Review "The Unity of Greek Medicine" in Chapter 2.)

The actual techniques used by Jesus and the New Testament Christians after him, were those of folklore medicine. A saliva mudpack was used on one occasion to cure blindness (John 9:6). Jesus healed a deaf-mute man by putting his finger in the man's ears, by putting his own saliva on the deaf-mute's tongue, and by pronouncing a special word, "Be opened" (Mark 7:33-34). In another case Jesus combined saliva treatment on the eyes with a special "laying on of hands" to heal a blind man (Mark 8:22-25). There are many instances of healing by touching or laying on of hands. These seem to be understood as a healing by transmission of power either from or through the healing person. (Review Chapter 4.) This even goes to the extremes of touching the healing person's clothing, as in the case of the woman with the flow of blood (Mark 6:25- 29), and the report that "handkerchiefs or aprons" of Paul were carried away to the sick "and diseases left them and evil spirits came out of them" (Acts 9:11). Even Peter's shadow was believed to be effective in healing those upon whom it fell (Acts 5:15).

Using the name of Jesus for healing also falls into the class of folklore healing methods. Peter healed the lame man "by the name of Jesus Christ of Nazareth" (Acts 3:6; 4:10). The disciples used the name to exorcise demons.

Ritual washing was used in curing the man born blind. After the saliva mudpack application, he was told "to wash in the pool of Siloam" and when he washed he came back seeing (John 9:7). The lame man by the pool Bethzatha believed that the waters had special healing powers, after being troubled by an angel (John 5:2-9).

There are also many instances of "faith-healings." (Review Chapter 3.) "Your faith has made you well" recurs several times in New Testament stories, in both of Jesus' healings and apostolic healings. In all these instances of folklore techniques for healing there is a general presupposition of divine power at work to effect the cure.

Other folkremedies seem to be not attached to any reliance on divine power. They are more closely related to the Hippocratic variety of Greek medicine (which seeks natural causes and cures) than to the Asklepian (which depends on supernatural powers). In the New Testament these folk remedies are not as common as the divine healing techniques, but they are there. Mark reports Jesus' disciples as using a healing technique of "anointing with oil many that were sick" (6:13). Oil is also recommended in the Epistle of James, although it is accompanied there by a religious ritual employing "the name of the Lord" and prayer (5:14). In 1 Timothy Paul instructs Timothy to "no longer drink only water, but use a little wine for the sake of your stomach and your frequent ailments" (5:23). Considering the condition of drinking water in those days, that bit of advice was probably quite sound!

Physicians in the New Testament

There is nothing in the New Testament resembling the professional physician of the first Christian century. Jesus once made a passing reference to those who are well not needing a physician (Mark 3:17), implying that those who are ill do need one; that's as close as the New Testament comes to professional physicians of the Hippocratic—that is, non-supernatural—type.

In Mark's story of the woman with the flow of blood, the Evangelist seems to be expressing a negative view of physicians, for the account says that she "had suffered much under many physicians, and had spent all that she had, and was no better but rather grew worse" (Mark 6:26). That sentiment of distrust in physicians is probably more characteristic of the New Testament's general preference for regarding healing as God's work rather than a human responsibility.

The Benefits of Illness

There is a certain acceptance of illness in the New Testament as functionally useful. It is sometimes regarded as purposeful and beneficial. Perhaps the most striking instance of this is the unknown malady of the Apostle Paul. He once called it his "thorn . . . in the flesh" (2 Cor. 12:7), and on another occasion "a bodily ailment" (Gal. 5:13). Thinking at first that it was "a messenger of Satan," he three times prayed that it should leave him, but it didn't. He seems to have finally concluded that it was purposeful, that in his weakness the power of God was made more visible or more perfect (2 Cor. 12:8-9).

For the most part, however, the New Testament regards illness and disease and even death as contrary to God's ultimate intention for human life. The New Testament vision of the Kingdom of God is one of an age to come when "God himself . . . will wipe away every tear . . . and death shall be no more, neither shall their be mourning nor crying nor pain any more, for the former things have passed away" (Rev. 21:4). Perhaps this vision of the ideal is a sufficient mandate for doing all that we can to move toward the fulfillment of complete healthiness.

12 What Is Spiritual Healthiness?

The spiritual healthiness question is first and essentially a question about humanity. It has to do with a special aspect of a human being. It deals with a more-or-less distinct attribute of a human being. It is only secondarily connected with theological questions. What God is like may be ultimately impossible for us humans to find out. To describe a human being is difficult enough. I prefer to approach our subject from the lesser of the two difficulties.

Defining a Human Being

What is a human being? We are a complex of many aspects. Some aspects are much more distinct and self-evident than others. What we are concerned with in this chapter is the least evident end of the continuum between the known and the unknown. The physical body is near the known end. With much yet to learn, the body is still the clearest, best known aspect of a human being. What we call the mind is also clearly evident in our own self-understanding, but its workings are much more of a mystery to us than the body's functioning. Our emotions are more obscure yet, with all the links being discovered between the emotions and both bodily and mental aspects of a human. But when we come to discuss the soul, or the spiritual aspect of a human being, we know least of all. There are many theories. We will begin with a brief description of the ancient ones that lie behind Western (European) thought.

The oldest ideas of which we are aware regarded a human being as a mind-emotion-body complex that was made alive by some outside power that departed when one died. Only a shadow of the person survived death, and if proscribed rituals were properly carried out, this shadow (or shade) entered forever, into "the Land of the Dead." This underground place was called Sheol by the Hebrews,

Tartarus by the Greeks, Anwat by the Egyptians, Orcus by the Romans, etc. This shade was not the essential human being, but only a shadow of the former self. The basic assumption of ancient Mediterranean cultures was that the human being was a mind-body complex, animated by a "spirit," and limited in time to the period between birth and death. The ancient Hebrews shared this concept with the ancient Near Eastern Mediterranean world.

Soon another concept appeared. It appeared earliest in India, but also somewhat later in Greece. This concept defined a human being as a non-physical "entity" (to use a modern term for didactic purposes) that was distinctly different from the body. "Soul" was a common way to designate this essential aspect of a human. The true self was the soul. In Indian (Hindu) theology the soul passed through an almost perpetual series of successive incarnations, without losing its personal identity. The real self could inhabit a human body or that of any other life form, from animal to insect.

The body and its functions are not part of the essential being. The body merely houses (temporarily) the real human being. In early Greek thought a similar idea goes back at least to Orphism. The Greek form powerfully influenced Western thought. Orphics regarded the essential human being as a naturally immortal soul, imprisoned temporarily in a mortal body.

Pythagoras adopted this Orphic concept and gave it a more solid philosophical setting. It achieved even more respectability when taught by Plato. From neo-Platonism this idea of a human being passed into early Christianity. The Orphic-Pythagorean-Platonic idea of a human being as a naturally immortal soul, imprisoned temporarily in a mortal body, is still well-entrenched in European thought, including Christianity. In this viewpoint, "soul" and "spirit" are interchangeable terms to describe the essential human being.

There were some Greeks who gave philosophical respectability to the older notions of a human being as a complex of body-soul-emotions-mind. Early materialists like Democritos failed to gain much of a following, and even Aristotle's adoption of the body-soul-mind unity of a human being did not dislodge the dominant Platonic concept, either in his own time or even after being adapted and adopted fifteen hundred years later by Thomas Aquinas! The immortal soul concept has prevailed to our own time!

Just prior to the rise of Christianity, there arose another viewpoint about what a human being is. According to it we are not a soul-body complex, nor are we a soul imprisoned in a physical body. Instead, we are essentially a spirit that is trapped within a body and a soul. This inner spirit is the essential human, and at the same time it is not human at all. It is a bit of the Divine Being, unfortunately detached from its source. This is the viewpoint of Gnosticism. According to the Gnostics we humans are, in essence, "sparks" (a favorite Gnostic term) of the divine, living in ignorance of who we really are and in ignorance of the true God, who is Spirit!

In summary, what are we human beings, according to ancient theories? We may be a complex unity in which the body is so integral that we cease to exist when the body dies. We may be naturally immortal souls imprisoned in a mortal body until death sets us free. We may be a part of God needing to be awakened to the knowledge of who we are and who God is. These are the three main ancient concepts, and they are still very much with us today.

Is there any new knowledge? Of course! Much new knowledge is available, mostly from the 20th century. It is surprising to me how this new knowledge seems to support the ancient theories!

What is the new knowledge? It comes from two sources. First, there is all the scientific medical research on the nerve system, the brain, and the glands that influence the chemistry of the body. This research is documenting the complex interrelations of bodily functions and our emotional and mental health. Very little has been done, as yet, to relate these findings to our spiritual condition. Many of the researchers are unable to separate the spiritual from the mental and emotional; so in a sense, this data is new knowledge yet to be assimilated to our special concern.

A second supply of new knowledge comes from the less-respected reports of data from extra-sensory sources. Careful research methods, critically applied, have helped to rescue this source of information from the folklore category. To understand what we are as human beings, I believe we must include all the data, rigorously tested, from whatever source. This, of course, is still a sensitive area, and some persons prefer to exclude all of this data as unreliable.

Having surveyed the classical viewpoints and admitted new data into the picture, what are the current options? There are three, and these are little more than updated versions of the three classical viewpoints.

Popular now is what is often called the holistic approach. This is substantially the old Hebraic viewpoint, minus the shade-survivor that goes to the Land of the Dead. Aristotle would probably be comfortable with this. Much of modern research from the sciences supports this. It ultimately makes traditional Christian beliefs in immortality and "life after death" difficult to maintain. What we are as human beings becomes increasingly difficult to imagine apart from the body, with its nerves, brain, and glands.

Bernard Reusch, in his recent book *Homo Sapiens*, is relentlessly logical in his holistic approach. He concludes that it is improbable that,

at some stage of the embryonic development between the fertilized germ cell and the infant at birth, something psychic, an individual soul, should arise as something fundamentally different from physiological processes, but also exhibiting characteristics of parents and ancestors[1]

Inheritance factors in our physical, mental and emotional aspects seem to me not only plausible but demonstrated. The same may be said of esthetic and artistic traits, but does

[1]Bernard Reusch, Homo Sapiens: *from man to demigod* (New York: Columbia Univ. Press, 1972), p. 200.

our so-called "soul" "exhibit characteristics of our parents and ancestors?" We have, as yet, no information on this.

A second modern option is an up-dating of the old Orphic-Pythagorean-Platonic viewpoint. The real human being is a non-physical entity occupying a body in this life. Related to many futile abortion discussions is the question of when the fetus becomes a human being. (When is the arrival or creation of the soul?) Augustine said it was 40 days after conception for males, and 90 days for females! There are many other such guesses.

The belief that a human being is a non-physical entity is sometimes coupled with a belief in the pre-existence of this entity. This belief, in turn, is usually coupled with a belief in the entity's post-existence. This life is thus only one of a series of incarnations of the human entity. This belief in reincarnation goes back to Pythagoras, at least. Hinduism and Buddhism and modern psychics like Edgar Cayce are likely to be more influential among contemporary defenders of this viewpoint than Pythagoras or Plato. Less reputable support comes from Scientology and similar cultish forms of religion.

A distinguished representative of those who believe that a human being is an immortal entity is Mircea Eliade of the University of Chicago. In his *The Sacred and the Profane* he says,

> Human life is not felt as a brief appearance in time, between one nothingness and another; it is preceded by a pre-existence and continued in a post-existence. Little is known about these two extra-terrestrial stages of human life, yet they are known to exists.[2]

Of course, exponents of rigorous holism, such as Bernard Reusch, would not agree that "they are known to exist."

A third modern option is a popular continuation of the ancient Gnostic viewpoint, with some adjustments. In this

---

[2]Mircea Eliade, *The Sacred and the Profane* (New York: Harcourt, Brace & World, Inc., 1959), p. 148.

understanding we humans are essentially detached bits of the divine reality. Temporary pressing demands and urges of the body tend to obscure what we really are. We humans are thus three-fold beings, rather than the two-fold beings of Orphic and Platonic assumptions. In modern adjustments of this three-fold understanding, older terms like soul and spirit, distinguished from each other in classical Gnostic anthropology, are now usually regarded as synonymous. We are body, mind, and soul/spirit. (Our emotions are usually appended to our mind-body complex in this viewpoint.) The soul/spirit is not merely naturally immortal; it is the very presence of the Eternal God. God is at the center of our being, and salvation lies in knowing that we and God are all one reality. This viewpoint is currently quite in vogue among spiritual formation writers.

In our quest for understanding what we are as human beings, I am ready to make the following conclusions:

1. All these viewpoints are finally a matter of personal opinion: The data available can be harmonized with each of these so-called "modern" options. All one can say is "I think such and such is what a human being is."

2. Next, each opinion has a certain validity. At our present state of knowledge, all we can do is to affirm as probable that we humans are body and non-body, that the two are intimately related, and that the non-body aspect includes mentality, emotions and other "feelings" which are different from thinking and different from emotions, and yet not independent of them. It is in the delineation of this non-body aspect that we have the most yet to learn.

Defining Spiritual Healthiness

Now we can turn to the task of defining what it means to be spiritually healthy. Prior to this question is another one: What does it mean to be healthy?

109

A. A negative definition: healthy means not being sick.
B. A functional definition: healthiness means everything is working properly.

Application of these definitions is easy in the case of our body, because its sickness is manifest in pain. The body is an organism which has functioning parts. When we feel well and the body seems to be functioning properly, we say we are physically healthy. Of course, we are already in trouble, because "dis-ease" sometimes doesn't manifest itself until well-advanced.

Application to our mental aspect is fairly easy, but now we are entering some really muddy waters. In the first place, we don't have the pain clues any more. We may talk about our "mental anguish" or "pain," but this usually refers to an emotional state and has little to do with the mental dimension of humanity. It is more a term to distinguish this kind of pain from neurological (nerve-based) pain. We have "headaches," but that's really physical and is experienced as physical (bodily) pain.

In the second place, mental functioning is not as clear-cut as bodily functioning. It is related in some way to the measure of mental ability we have. To function poorly, for example, might be a symptom of poor mental health or simply low mental ability.

Finally, those who specialize in mental health do not fully agree on the traits of mental healthiness. It is beyond the scope of these reflections to review all these formulations, but at least there are some. One from the Menningers might well point us in the direction of a useful definition. They say mentally healthy persons have five basic traits:

1. They have a wide variety of sources of gratification.
2. They are flexible under stress; they can roll with the punches, and see alternative solutions to problems.
3. They recognize and accept their own limitations and their own strengths and assets; they see themselves accurately as they are and are satisfied with themselves.

110

4. They treat other persons as individuals; they listen to others and are genuinely interested in them; they are not preoccupied with themselves.
5. They are active and productive: they are in charge of themselves and control their activities, rather than being controlled by them.[3]

We enter even murkier waters when we try to define emotional health. Of course, we can avoid the problem if we decide not to make a distinction between mental and emotional. Granted that they are closely related—even intertwined—it still seems to most persons that mental has to do with a different aspect of a human being than emotional. It is in their purer forms that we can most easily recognize their separateness. Solving a puzzle seems to be a very different experience than grieving over the death of a loved one. But given the difference, what marks emotional healthiness? I can only raise the difficulty; to attempt an answer would carry us into another set of speculations and involve us in more disagreements than the mental health question.

Now, at last, we come to our main concern: What is spiritual health? By beginning with the more easily defined physical health aspect of a human being and going through the mental, emotional, and spiritual aspects, we have been coming closer and closer to the unknown. We don't really know what spiritual healthiness is.

The whole problem can be avoided by regarding the non-body aspects of a human as a unity which can't be separated into mental, emotional and spiritual. This is the viewpoint of psychiatrist, M. Scott Peck, in his book *The Road Less Traveled*. Behind this uniting of the non-physical aspects, especially the mental and spiritual, in the case of Dr. Peck, lies a very broad view of religion. Religion, for Peck, is simply how one understands what life is all about. He has no provision for one's understanding being secular,

---

[3]From Harry Levinson, *Men, Management*, and *Mental Health*, pp. 17-18.

111

or, as Mercea Eliade would say, "profane." Everyone, Peck insists, has some kind of world view, whether explicitly understood or not (more commonly not, he says), and that is one's religion. He labels the narrower view of what's religious "simplistic," but I would tend to use the same word for his broad definition.[4]

Just as mental and emotional are commonly recognized as separate but interrelated, so there are other experiences that seem to be neither mental or emotional in their "essence." For example, one is sometimes aware of the presence of another person, but this awareness is not perceived through the physical senses. This is an experience not obviously related to the mind and, while often having emotional consequences, does not seem to arise out of emotional sources either. Such experiences are more closely related to intuition than to reason or emotion.

If I am right in giving this aspect its own identity, we can then proceed to examine the question of how this real area of experience may be perceived as healthy or unhealthy. For convenience I will adopt the traditional terminology for our quest, leaving behind the questions of mental and emotional health, and calling our focus-area the area of the spiritual. This conforms more closely to Gnostic anthropology than to Greek or Hebrew, but carries the three-fold Gnostic anthropology (body-soul-spirit to a further level of complexity, with a four-fold anthropology of body-mind-emotion-spirit. I will also treat the words "soul" and "spirit as virtually identical (following some of the Greeks). This will agree with the popular usage of these words. To do serious biblical exegesis or research into the history of ideas about what a human being is, one would need to use these terms with more precision.

We should remember that all the healths of a human being are interrelated. Some points of interrelationship are so strong as to be causal. That is, some physical conditions

---

[4]M. Scott Peck, *The Road Less Traveled* (New York: Simon and Schuster, 1978), pp. 185-6.

can cause poor mental health or poor emotional health. I suspect that this extends also to spiritual health, but I know of no research to establish this. (The very idea is heretical for many persons.) Whether causal or not, the interrelations are at least influential.

One might, therefore, begin the quest for a definition of spiritual health by claiming the necessity (or, at least, the helpfulness) of good health in all the other areas of a human being. But this doesn't really define spiritual healthiness: it just defines the environment within which it usually happens. But what is it, in itself?

My own study of this topic began when I realized that I already had a definition of spiritually healthy persons, namely this one: A spiritually healthy person is a person like me. Anyone who differed markedly from my own spirituality was suspect. I tended to regard such a deviant as unhealthy. Of course, that was an unexamined assumption and quite indefensible. How could I be the standard for judgment? So I began searching for something more objective. I searched first in the books on spirituality, both the classics and the moderns. I found little help here, because these writers weren't asking my question. Each one had his or her own unexamined assumptions (usually just like mine!). In fact, the terminology of health is not the traditional way to discuss spirituality.

I did get some help from the psychological classic of William James, *The Varieties of Religious Experience*. He distinguished between a certain kind of piety labeled "sick" and another labeled "healthy."[5]

For Dr. James (whose terminology, at least, roots back into the mid-nineteenth century in the writings of Francis W. Newman) spiritually healthy persons are marked by "irreclaimable" happiness. They feel the goodness of life; they are at peace with themselves and the universe and

---

[5]William James, *The Varieties of Religious Experience*, New York: Longmans, Green, and Co., 1915. Lectures IV and V; VI and VII.

God. They are the "once-born" and do not experience "religious struggles" or see life as "a problem." Their optimism may, James recognizes, become "quasi-pathological;" but then, as Milton observed,[6] any virtue, carried too far, becomes a vice. James selected Walt Whitman as "the supreme contemporary example" of this healthy-minded "inability to feel evil."[7] James quotes these lines from Whitman's "Song of Myself" in *Leaves of Grass:*

> I could turn and live with animals, they are so
>   placid and self-contained,
> I stand and look at them long and long;
>
> They do not sweat and whine about their
>   condition,
> They do not lie awake in the dark and weep for
>   their sins,
> They do not make me sick discussing their duty to God,
> Not one is dissatisfied, not one is demented with
>   the mania of owning things,
> Not one kneels to another, nor to his kind that
>   lived thousands of years ago,
> Not one is respectable or unhappy over the whole
>   earth.[8]

And again Walt Whitman says, "what is called good is perfect and what is called bad is just as perfect."[9] In this kind of spirituality, one looks in vain for a broken and contrite heart. "Repentance . . . means *getting away from* the sin, not groaning and writhing over its commission"[10] James quotes the Jesuit Molinos, calling him "that spiritual genius,"[11] to the effect that when we fall, we should have "a loving confidence in the divine mercy" and get up and go on.

---

[6]John Milton, *Areopagitica.*
[7]James, *The Varieties of Religious Experience*, p. 83.
[8]Op. cit., p. 85.
[9]Op. cit., p. 86.
[10]Op. cit., p. 126.
[11]Op. cit., p. 128.

In contrast, James describes as religiously "sick" those persons who maximize the evil aspects of existence. They have "a morbid way" of looking at life. They see the ills of the world and take them seriously. They struggle to cope with "the problem of evil," the sorrows and pains of life, and see death itself as the enemy. They reach out for answers to questions not even asked by the spiritually "healthy." These sick souls need to be "born-again:" they die to this life and this world to be born again in a new one. James himself concluded that this twice-born type of spirituality was closer to historic Christianity (and to his own liking).

That these understandings have a measure of truth in them may help to account for the continuing demand for his book; very few turn-of-the-century psychology books are still in print!

Helpful as Professor James is in our quest, he fails to address a basic question. He assumes that "spirituality" and "being religious" are the same. Does spirituality necessarily involve one in religion? Is there such a thing as secular spirituality? Does spiritual healthiness necessarily require acknowledgment of, even participation in, religious beliefs or practices or both? I'm inclined to give a negative answer to these questions.

This is the very point where the "spiritual masters" disappoint me. The classic works on spiritual formation, and most of the modern treatments of this topic, proceed on the unexamined assumption that spirituality and religion (usually Christianity) necessarily go together. That they often do go together is obviously true. But that they must go together is a moot point. If they must go together, then only religious people can be healthy spiritually. I would hesitate a long time before coming to that conclusion.

My hesitation begins when I contemplate non-Christian spirituality, such as that of Rabbi Abraham Heschel or Rabbi Leo Baeck. Personal experience with these great teachers has impressed me with the healthiness of their spirituality. But, as Jews, they were religious, of course. It's just that my provincially Christian way of dealing with religion broke down, and the role of "Christ" began to take on a relative status, rather than an absolute one.

Then I reflected on other religions and their connection with a "healthy" spirituality. Many of these are religious in our sense, and they pose no threat to the assumption we are examining other than to clarify our Christian provincialism. But this path leads to atheistic religions with spiritually healthy persons, and on to secular religions like some claim communism to be. The path brings us back into our culture, with its representatives of non-religious persons with healthy lives, people who seem to be "spiritually" healthy also.

Further complications come from the obvious fact that, by any definition of spiritual healthiness, there are quite a lot of super-religious persons who are, in my judgment, sick souls. Religious books abound. How much of spiritual unhealthiness is rooted in religion itself?

Suppose I tentatively allowed a person to be judged spiritually healthy if he or she had a sense of "at peace-ness" with the universe? What kind of definition would emerge? "At peace-ness" could be religious and even provincially religious, or it could be non-religious. In both cases it would be something other than a willful, mental decision. It would be more an unexplainable awareness, which could then be clothed in the garments of any religion, or of no religion at all.

I have a different approach to suggest. When we reflect on our physical health, we could define ourselves as healthy if nothing in our body is calling attention to itself. This is a flawed definition, of course, but in general it serves well. If we are living in practical oblivion of how healthy our body is, then it's healthy. To be too health-conscious is not healthy.

Now I'm going to propose that we try the same standard on the other "healths." If our mind is not calling special attention to itself, perhaps it's "healthy." If we are too-conscious of mental problems, perhaps we are not mentally healthy. If our emotions are not creating problems for us, perhaps we are emotionally healthy. If we are too-conscious of our emotional state, perhaps we are not in good emotional health. And so we come to spiritual healthiness. If we are untroubled by spiritual problems, perhaps we are in good spiritual health. If we are too conscious of spiritual problems, perhaps we are not spiritually healthy.

I'm suggesting that one dimension of our quest for a definition comes from the possibility of hypochondriac symptoms. Physical hypochondriacs are usually easy to identify. We sometimes talk behind their backs about their "organ-recitals." Are there spiritual hypochondriacs?

But we have to modify this. Left alone, sheer apathy would qualify for a healthy label. Perhaps it's more a matter of balance. Some concern for health is healthy. Too much is not.

Now the problem resolves into how much is too much? I don't know the answer to this. I'm just proposing that good spiritual health is probably indicated when one is in a condition that intrinsically draws one's attention away from the subject of our own spiritual healthiness.

Another way of saying the same thing is to repeat this standard of "being at peace" with one's self and one's surroundings. In Leslie Weatherhead's words, we have healthy spirits or souls (he uses the terms interchangeably) when we have a "harmonious relationship with the other parts" of our "personality, and its relevant environment."[12] A more complicated version of this is stated by Samuel H. Miller, who defines religion as a "symbolic structure" that is healthy when it provides us with a way of living comfortably with the mysteries of our existence.[13]

But now we have gone full circle and are back to what William James has popularized as healthy-mindedness in religion. All three (Weatherhead, Miller, and James) link spiritual healthiness with religion. I think there are many

---

[12]Leslie Weatherhead, *Psychology, Religion, and Health* (London: Hodder and Stoughton, 1952), p. 313.

[13]Samuel H. Miller, "Religion: Healthy and Nonhealthy," in the *Journal of Religion and Health*, Vol. 4, No. 4 (July, 1965).

spiritually healthy persons whose lives are comfortably "at peace" without a religious factor at all. After all there is at least a germ of truth in the observation of Ralph Waldo Emerson's friend: "Being perfectly well-dressed gives a feeling of tranquility that religion is powerless to bestow."

I think we arrived back here because that's where I am. I may not have gotten very far away from my own starting point: spiritually healthy persons are persons like me.

13 Cultivating Spiritual Healthiness?

The previous chapter focused on the human side of spirituality. We found differing concepts of a human being and of what spiritual healthiness is. We now turn to another formidable inquiry. How does one's spirituality relate to God or whatever it is that nurtures a healthy spiritual life? God was involved in our previous inquiry also, but now God is more central to the discussion.

The Difficulties

I confess I don't know how to get any data about God. We can claim that spiritual formation in a human being is the product of God-activity (whether acknowledged by the human or not). If we make this claim, then God-activity becomes an important object of our inquiry. But it is an impossible quest for us; we can only speculate.

A young computer designer, the founder of Apple computers, has helped me to understand my problem here. He expressed it this way, as quoted in a *Newsweek* interview:

> When you want to understand something that's never been understood before, what you have to do is construct a conceptual scaffolding. And if you're trying to design a computer you will literally immerse yourself in the thousands of details necessary; all of a sudden, as the scaffolding gets set up high enough, it will become clearer and clearer and that's when the breakthrough starts. It is a rhythmic experience, or it is an experience where everything's related to everything else and it's all intertwined. And it's such a fragile, delicate experience that it's very much like music. But you could never describe it to anyone.[1]

My attachment to music helps me to grasp this approach. Music can only be experienced; it cannot be explained. God

---

[1]*Newsweek*, Special Issue, Fall, 1984.

is like that. In an article on mysticism, John Wright Buckham acknowledges that "nowhere does mysticism find more complete expression than in music. Bach is one of the purest and most ardent of Christian mystics."[2]

More difficult for most persons than the music analogy is the Pythagorean concept of numbers, and I mention this only to underscore our difficulty. When the Pythagoreans understood numbers as true realities, as abstractions real in themselves, they took what Gardner Murphy calls a decisive "step away from sensory reality" (which is always unable to reach God) and a significant "step toward some other kind of reality" (one closer to a God-reality—perhaps).[3] This should make very clear the difficulty of the spiritual development quest.

The Task

The task before us needs further explanation. What we are about is the nuts and bolts of how to develop a healthy spirituality, a "how-to" manual, if you please. What practical difficulties lie in the way?

Dr. James Fowler would speak up here and say that it depends on our present stage of faith development as individuals. A person at one stage needs a different "how-to" manual than one at another. What is common to the needs of persons in all stages is the role that "cognitive dissonance" plays in helping us as individuals to move through the stages. And, of course, "cognitive" is not the only kind of dissonance we need to keep growing. We need experiential dissonances, as illustrated by John Wesley's change in attitude toward the Quakers. He thought they weren't Christian until he met one who was!

Another practical difficulty we encounter is the new discoveries about right-brain/left-brain factors in human

---

[2]In V. Ferm, editor, *Encyclopedia of Religion* (New York: Philosophical Library, 1945), p. 514a.

[3]Gardner Murphy, *Psychological Thought from Pythagoras to Freud* (New York: Harcourt, Brace & World, Inc., 1968), p. 17.

life. Spirituality traits for a primarily right-brain person are not the same as those for a primarily left-brain person. Experts in this field tell us that we aren't stuck in one category; we can develop into "whole-brain" persons, with a corresponding development in our spirituality traits.

An earlier expression of these individual differences, more generally expressed, is in the now-classic theories of William James in his *Varieties of Religious Experience*, already utilized for a different purpose in the previous chapter. The theory of James is simply that different personality types need different religions. Translated into terms of our inquiry, this affirms that spiritual formation procedures must be adapted to personality types. How one defines these types, and how many types one isolates, is irrelevant to the main point James made with his two types.

A final practical difficulty lies in the common experience of most persons, that we experience "seasons" in our spiritual life. We do not live on an even keel. For some reason, or reasons, we have our ups and our downs, spiritually. The greatest of the spiritual leaders confess that they experience what St. John of the Cross called "the dark night of the soul." Our up-stages seem to require a different path than our down-stages.

Having looked at these difficulties that complicate our task, we can now plunge recklessly ahead. Retrospective historical scholarship reveals to me two rival approaches to our task, and we will examine each of these.

The Way of the Will

What first calls itself to our attention I choose to call "The Way of the Will." This is a way of personal, willfully chosen discipline. It is a striving way, an earnest endeavor. In the language of the Pastoral Epistles, it is to "wage the good warfare" (1 Tim. 1:18). It is to

train yourself in godliness; for while bodily training is of some value, godliness is of value in every way, as it holds promise for the present life and also for the life to come (I Tim. 4:76-8).

No soldier on service gets entangled in civilian pursuits, since his aim is to satisfy the one who enlisted him. An athlete is not crowned unless he competes according to the rules. It is the hard-working farmer who ought to have the first share of the crops (2 Tim. 2:4-6).

This strenuous effort of the will to move toward somekind of spiritual perfection came to full flower in the monastic movement of Catholic Christianity, both Greek and Latin. The stabilization of Latin monasticism by Benedict, the rise of the Dominicans and Franciscans, and especially the stringent rules of the Jesuits gave Roman Catholicism one of its classical patterns for Christian formation, a pattern I am labeling Type A. It is emphatically a "Way of the Will," a questing after holiness by following a severely disciplined life. Ignatius Loyola's Spiritual Exercises informs the reader that although we use the mind when reasoning, "in acts of the will . . . greater reverence is required on our part."[4] The *Spiritual Exercises* themselves are quite detailed and are intended to give direction to "the ordering of one's life with a view to the salvation of one's soul."[5]

Contemporary with Loyola was Teresa of Avila, prioress of a Carmelite Monastery for nuns and author of two classics in Roman Catholic monastic spirituality (her autobiography and her *Mansions of the Interior Castle*). Teresa wrote glowingly about the possession of perfect love. "If we aspire to the perfect possession of this true love of God, it brings all blessings with it."[6] We "attain" this supreme blessing by a complete surrendering to God of our own importance and our desires for earthly things. It is hard to surrender to God completely. Only a few are able to do this. "So," she says, "being unable to make a full surrender

---

[4]In C. Manschreck, *A History of Christianity* (Englewood Cliffs, N.J.: Prentice-Hall, Inc., 1964), vol. II, p. 119.
[5]Ibid.
[6]*The Life of St. Teresa of Avila* (translated by E. Allison Peers) (London: Sheed and Ward, 1979), p. 63.

of ourselves, we are never given a full supply of this treasure."[7] She then asserts:

> The Lord shows exceeding great mercy to him whom He gives grace and courage to resolve to strive after this blessing with all his might. For God denies Himself to no one who perseveres, but gradually increases the courage of such a one till he achieves victory.[8]

This is a beautifully representative statement of "The Way of the Will." It calls to mind the central piety of the Hebrew scriptures, as expressed, for example, in the familiar verse given its classical expression and musical setting by Mendelssohn in his oratorio *Elijah*: "If with all your hearts ye truly seek me, ye shall surely find me; thus saith the Lord" (based on Jer. 29:13). In this classical (Type A) pattern of spiritual formation, God is hidden somewhere and we must actively seek God out; if we seek diligently enough, we shall surely find God. God is available to the energetic, dedicated seeker. As Teresa says, "God denies Himself to no one who perseveres."[9]

This God-quest is closely related to an area of spiritual formation that experiences "ecstasies" or "God-encounters" that lie at the heart of Christian forms of mysticism. The Christian mystics experience what they understand to be union with God. They find it notoriously difficult to describe in words what this experience is, but they value it above all other experiences. Teresa, after years of striving, had experiences even beyond mystical union, experiences which she calls "ecstasies" and "raptures." In her early forties these included out-of-body experiences and levitation. She witnessed that these raptures were even more sublime than mystical union. She clearly regarded these as gifts of God, not achievements of her will, but the gifts were God's response to her willful surrender of herself.

---

[7]Op. cit., p. 64.
[8]Ibid.
[9]Ibid.

Teresa's understanding of these ecstasies went beyond mere union with God. She felt a moment at the climax of the rapture when her soul was transformed into God. This comes very close to the divinization theology of Greek orthodoxy, in which the goal of spiritual formation is for the human to become divine, as expressed in 2 Peter 1:4 and the Orthodox Western Eucharistic liturgy, to "become partakers of the divine nature." The metaphysical anthropology behind Teresa's mysticism is fundamentally Orphic; she speaks freely about the soul as the body's prisoner.

Another exponent of "The Way of the Will," in a very different setting and in a very different age, is our recurring helper, William James. He had serious physical health problems. His years at Harvard were plagued by much suffering. On his journeys to Germany he experienced severe backaches, eyeaches, and headaches. During one of his health crises, he read a work by the French philosopher Charles Renouvier and discovered the importance of the role of the will in his own sufferings. James willed to live as a well man, and his health radically improved. Out of this came his famous essay "The Will to Believe," in which he asserted that a willfully chosen belief "may bring into existence a reality which cannot otherwise be."[10] From this stance he defended the "mind healers" of Boston in the suit brought against them by orthodox physicians. This, of course, is the period of early Christian Science and its belief in the power of the mind to heal physical ills.

In our own time one immediately thinks of Norman Cousins. He too healed himself by willing it. He has influenced many by his articles and especially his book *The Healing Heart*.

Norman Vincent Peale also comes to mind with his *Power of Positive Thinking*. All these examples serve to illustrate, in very different forms, an underlying commitment to the power of the will to achieve healthiness, whether of body or soul.

---

[10]Gardner Murphy, op. cit., p. 146.

What strikes me again is the unconscious assumptions of Gnosticism that are usually present in Type A spirituality. Central to Gnosticism is the belief that humans are essentially sparks of the divine. The human spirit needs most of all to be re-connected with God, the big Spirit. This central idea is also expressed in most of these Type A spiritual formation patterns, often in Johannine-Gnostic forms, such as the unity of God, Christ, and the believer in John 17 and elsewhere. It is the essence of the now popular "journey-inward" language and some of the "centering" talk. It is deep within our own being that we will find God. Henri Nouwen says, "The development of this inner sensitivity is the beginning of a spiritual journey."[11] "The spiritual life is a reaching out to our innermost self."[12] This is the essence of the Jungian psychology of spirituality.

Teresa of Avila, in her *Interior Castle*, imagines the human soul as a large castle, with seven concentric circles of rooms; in the innermost room is God. I was surprised, to say the least, to find it even in the Reform Jewish Prayer Book: "We believe that the spiritual reality within us corresponds to a spiritual reality beyond us, and in worship w hope to bring the two realities into communion."[13] The Gospel of John, that least Jewish of the Gospels, could hardly say it better!

What is surprising, further, is that this hidden Gnostic spirituality is adopted within a non-Gnostic framework of striving and earnest endeavor of the will. The Gospel of John does not make that connection. In it, we "become children of God not . . . of the will of man but of God" (John 1:13).

This Type A classical Christian spirituality is the kind that gets the most attention in spiritual formation circles. It is by far the most popular type, with more instruction books, manuals, witnesses, formulas and the like than the other main type to which we shall now turn.

---

[11]Henri Nouwen, *Reaching Out* (Garden City, N.Y.: Doubleday & Co., Inc., 1975), p. 26.
[12]Op. Cit., p. 9.
[13]Teresa, *The Interior Castle*, Introduction, XI.

The Way of the Princes of Serendip

I choose to call the other main type of classical spiritual formation by the label, "The Way of the Princes of Serendip." It is Type B. My label, of course, comes from Horace Walpole's story of the three traveling princes of Serendip who make interesting discoveries accidentally, while aiming for something else. This story is also the source of the new word "serendipity." Type B spiritual formation understands spirituality as a by-product of doing something else.

One analogy that comes to mind is the source of happiness in life. Happiness is an elusive value; the more one pursues it, the more it flees away. But when one ignores it, and busies oneself in worthwhile and helpful activities, happiness comes sneaking in the back door to surprise us.

Another beginning analogy is the special quality of child-like naivete. That's not something one can cultivate, or get by striving. It's a non-self-conscious quality that vanishes when attention is turned inward toward it. Naive child-likeness is an "age of innocence" which not only vanishes when self-examined, but becomes positively destroyed by deliberate educational disciplines. Incidentally, that's why "babes in the faith" find their religious beliefs destroyed by education. Hence the distrust of higher education among those who are still "babes." But, of course, education is not the enemy of the faith and the destroyer of spiritual formation; it is the dynamic that moves us into more complex stages of faith and helps us to hold on to the faith in a world no longer naively innocent.

Enough of imperfect analogies. As a prime example of the very antithesis of Teresa of Avila, let us examine the spirituality of Simone Weil. Andre Gide ranks her as "the most truly spiritual writer of this century."[14] T. S. Eliot

---

[14]Comment on the dust jacket of Simone Weil's book *Waiting For God* (New York: Harper & Row, 1951).

wrote that her last post-humously published book was "almost too important to be include in one's list of preferred reading for one year only."[15] Simone Weil is a twentieth century master of Greek and the Greek classics. Reared in a Jewish home, she became a Roman Catholic Christian by choice in all but the formalities. She experienced "being possessed by Christ" in a setting that she felt was none of her own doing. She had great empathy for the working classes and struggled during most of her 34 years with serious physical health problems.

Like many of the earlier Roman Catholic women mystics, she wrote of her Christ-encounter in terms of "being possessed by Christ." She used the language of love that lends itself equally to spiritual and earthly loves. With her passion for truth, she joined together her truth-quests with her Christ-encounter, in this fashion:

> One can never wrestle enough with God if one does so out of pure regard for the truth. Christ likes us to prefer truth to him, because, before being Christ, he is truth. If one turns aside from him to go toward the truth, one will not go far before falling into his arms.[16]

How did Simone Weil understand this way of spirituality? What are its dynamics? She believed it was God's initiative, not ours. She wrote,

> The attitude that brings us salvation is not like any form of activity. The Greek word which expresses it is *hypomené*, and *patientia* is rather an inadequate translation of it. It is the waiting or attentive and faithful immobility that last indefinitely and cannot be shaken.
>
> Active searching is prejudicial. . . . Seeking leads us astray. This is the case with every form of what is truly good . . . true virtue in every domain is negative. . . . This waiting . . . is, however, something more intense than searching.

---

[15]Ibid.
[16]*Waiting For God*, p. 69.

127

She goes on to say,

> The notion of grace, as opposed to virtue depending on the will, and that of inspiration, as opposed to intellectual or artistic work, these two notions, if they are well understood, show the efficacy of desire and of waiting.
>
> Attention animated by desire is the whole foundation of religious practices. . . .[17]

Of course, she does not mean passive waiting at all. One only needs to look at her life to know that she understood that we should be busy serving while waiting. As she also wrote in her *Waiting for God:*

> It would . . . be more in conformity with the spirit of Christianity if . . . Christ went to bring his presence into those places most polluted with shame, misery, crime, and affliction, into prisons and law courts, into work-houses and shelters for the wretched and the outcast.[18]

But still, it is while we are busy with these things that our spirituality is developed. Service does not automatically hallow a person; that person must desire what is being waited for, Weil said, and that waiting and desiring are "something more intense than any searching."[19]

Now it will be easy to describe the Type B pattern of spiritual formation in more conventional and orthodox language. "Main-line" Christianity has, for centuries, dealt with spiritual formation by teaching that we can only wait in the means of grace. This stems back to the early Catholic Church's modified adoption of the understanding found in our earliest extant Christian writings, the letters of Paul, and the later variant expressions of a similar understanding. These are the framework of Mark's Gospel, the Fourth Gospel, Colossians and Ephesians, 1 Peter, and Hebrews.

---

[17]Op. cit., p. 196-7.
[18]Op. cit., p. 198.
[19]Op. cit., p. 197.

The common denominator of these early understandings is an assumption of human helplessness and the good news of Christ as God's rescue act. We are rescued by the grace of God. Our salvation is not our own accomplishment.

This grace-theology, when properly understood, both enables and inspires good works. Thus one must always remember that the waiting for God in the means of grace does not mean inactivity or stagnation or paralysis, but one "waits" for the Lord in certain activities. These activities are those which, in the Church's experience, increase the chances of being rescued. God is still in full control, and these activities by no means carry a guarantee. Yet it is the witness of the Church (in its orthodox forms) that being in the means of grace is all we can do.

My only problem with this comes when the activities identified as means of grace are too narrowly defined. Conventional identifications of these potentially grace-full activities include participation in both public worship and private devotions, hearing, reading, studying scripture, prayer, preaching, Christian fellowship, and serving others. As we do these things, our spiritual life will be formed and will grow toward maturity.

This church-oriented pattern of activities defining the means of grace is too narrow. My first addition would be music, and music quite beyond the "sacred music" of the hymns and anthems of public worship. My spiritual life is nourished by so-called "secular" music as well, and "secular" drama and "secular" art and "secular" relationships with other humans. I have found that the so-called secular world has many times been, for me, "the means of grace." As a Prince of Serendip, I would sometimes wait for God merely in the presence of a "significant other," or in activities that the Church would traditionally label secular. I encourage an openness to the revelation of God's presence in the midst of activities not usually classified as a means of grace, as well as the traditional ones.

Both Carl Jung and Mircea Eliade have helped me to realize that symbols function somewhat like this. Eliade says that the sanctified life happens when one participates in the mythical symbols of the sacred world. To experience belonging to the sacred world is the hallmark of the religious person. To live in sacred space and in sacred time, as these are symbolized for us, is the essence of the spiritual life. But all this spiritual development is a "happening," not a product of our strenuous striving. Eliade notes that we become "aware of the sacred because **it** manifests **itself**."[20] This manifestation is "of something of a wholly different order, a reality that does not belong to our world."[21] Symbols of nature, its "cosmic rhythms" are the means of grace for Eliade; we "need only decipher what the cosmos says in its many modes of being," and we "will understand the mystery of life."[22] This deciphering is not a mental or spiritual task; it comes to us, we know not how. As for me, personally, I am closer to being a Prince of Serendip than a Spiritual Exerciser.

Conclusion

Now I want to modify both Type A and Type B. The truth is more complex than either type by itself. Type A, the earnest endeavor approach, is always, at its best, conscious of the giftness of our spiritual well-being. Type B, the waiting for God approach, is, at its best, always busy in worthwhile activities. We should work as though it all depends on us, and pray as though it all depends on God. Perhaps that's as close as we can come to a formula for keeping our spiritual life in good health.

---

[20]Mircea Eliade, *The Sacred and the Profane* (New York: Harcourt, Brace & World, Inc., 1959), p. 11.
[21]Ibid.
[22]Op. cit., p. 148.

BIBLIOGRAPHY

Books marked with a double asterisk are highly recommended by the author.

A Century of Christian Science Healing. Boston: The Christian Science Publishing Society, 1966.

Althouse, Lawrence W. *Rediscovering the Gift of Healing*. Nashville: Abingdon Press, 1977.

Barrett, C. K. *Luke the Historian in Recent Study*. Philadelphia: Fortress Press, 1970. (Facet Books: Biblical Series No. 24, revision of 1961 lecture).**

Buckham, John Wright, "Mysticism" in V Form, ed., *Encyclopedia of Religion*, New York: Philosophical Library, 1946.

Campbell, Joseph. *Myths to Live By*. New York: Viking, 1972.

Christ, Carol P. and Judith Plaskow, eds. *Womanspirit Rising*. San Francisco: Harper and Row, 1979.

Clinebell, Howard John, ed. *Community Mental Health*. Nashville: Abingdon Press, 1970.

Conzelmann, Hans. *An Outline of the Theology of the New Testament*. 2nd edition. Trans. John Bowden. New York: Harper and Row, 1969.**

Conzelmann, Hans. *The Theology of St. Luke*. Trans. Geoffrey Buswell. London: Faber and Faber, 1960.

Cousins, Norman. *Anatomy of an Illness*. 1979; rpt. New York: Bantam, 1981.

Creed, John Martin. *The Gospel According to Luke*. London: Macmillan and Co., 1930.**

Danker, Frederick W. *Jesus and the New According to St. Luke: A Commentary on the Third Gospel*. St. Louis: Clayton, 1972.

Danker, Frederick W. *Luke*. Philadelphia: Fortress Press, 1976.

Dibelius, Martin. *Studies in the Acts of the Apostles*, ed. H. Greeven. Trans. Mary Ling. New York: Scribner's, 1956.**

Easton, Burton Scott. *Early Christianity: The Purpose of Acts and other Papers*. London: S.P.C.K., 1955.

Ebon, Martin. *The Devil's Bride. Exorcism: Past and Present*. New York: Harper and Row, 1974.

Eliade, Mircea. *The Sacred and the Profane*, New York: Harcourt, Brace & World, Inc., 1959.**

Ellis, Earle E. *Eschatology in Luke*. Philadelphia: Fortress Press, 1972.

131

Emswiler, Thomas Neufer and Sharon Neufer Emswiler. *Wholeness in Worship*. San Francisco: Harper and Row, 1980.**

Fichter, Joseph H. *Religion and Pain*. New York: Crossroad, 1981.

Franklin, Eric. *Christ the Lord: A Study in the Purpose and Theology of Luke-Acts*. Philadelphia: Westminster, 1975.

Frazier, Claude A. Ed. *Healing and Religious Faith*. Philadelphia: United Church Press, 1974.

Fuller, John G. *Arigo: Surgeon of the Rusty Knife*. New York: Thomas Y. Crowell Co., 1974.**

Giles, Mary E. Ed. *The Feminist Mystic*. New York: Crossroad, 1982.

Goldwag, Elliott M. Ed. *Inner Balance: The Power of Holistic Healing*. Englewood Cliffs: Prentice-Hall, 1979.**

Goodman, Felicitas D. *The Exorcism of Anneliese Michel*. New York: Doubleday and Co., 1981.**

Haenchen, Ernst. *The Acts of the Apostles*. Trans. from the 14th edition of the German under the supervision of Hugh Anderson. Rev. by R. Mc. L. Wilson. Philadelphia: Westminster, 1971.**

Jackson, F. J. Foakes and Kirsopp Lake, eds. *The Beginnings of Christianity*, Part I, The Acts of the Apostles (5 vols). London: MacMillan and Co., 1933.**

James, William. *The Varieties of Religious Experience*. (1902; many subsequent printings; I used the Modern Library edition, no date, from Random House), Lectures IV, V, VI, and VII.**

Jeremias, Joachim. *The Parables of Jesus*. Revised Edition. Trans. S. H. Hooke. New York: Charles Scribner's Sons, 1963.**

Keck, Leander E. and J. Louis Martyn. Eds. *Studies in Luke-Acts*. Nashville: Abingdon Press, 1966.**

Kelsey, Morton T. *Healing and Christianity in Ancient Thought and Modern Times*. New York: Harper and Row, 1973.**

Krieger, Dolores. *The Therapeutic Touch*. Englewood Cliffs, New Jersey: Prentice-Hall, 1980.**

Kuhlman, Kathryn. *God Can Do It Again*. Englewood Cliffs, New Jersey: Prentice-Hall, 1969.

Kuhlman, Kathryn. *Nothing is Impossible with God*. Englewood Cliffs, New Jersey: Prentice-Hall, Inc., 1974.

Leslie, Robert C. *Health Healing and Holiness*. Nashville: Graded Press, 1971.**

Lhermitte, Jean. *True and False Possession*. Trans. New York: Hawthorn Books, 1963.

Linn, Matthew, S.J., and Dennis Linn, S.J. *The Healing of Memories*. New York: Paulist Press, 1974.

MacLeod, George. *The Place of Healing in the Ministry of the Church*. Glasgow Scotland: The Iona Community Publishing Department, n.d.**

MacNutt, Francis. *Healing*. Indiana: Ave Maria Press, 1974.**

MacNutt, Francis. *The Power to Heal*. Notre Dame, Indiana: Ave Maria Press, 1977.**

Manschreck, C. *A History of Christianity*. Vol. II. Englewood Cliffs, New Jersey: Prentice-Hall, Inc., 1964.

Marty, Martin E. and Kenneth L. Vaux. Eds. *Health/Medicine and the Faith Traditions; An Inquiry into Religion and Medicine*. Philadelphia: Fortress Press, 1982.**

Miller, Samuel H. "Religion: Healthy and Nonhealthy," in *Journal of Religion and Health*, Vol. 4, No. 4. July, 1965.

Milton, John. "Areopagitica".

Montagu, Ashley. *Touching: The Human Significance of the Skin*. New York: Columbia University Press, 1971.

Murphy, Gardner. *Psychological Thought from Pythagoras to Freud*. New York: Harcourt, Brace & World, Inc., 1968.

Newsweek, Special Issue, Fall, 1984.

Nineham, Dennis. *The Use and Abuse of the Bible*. London: Macmillan, 1976.**

Nouwen, Henri. *Reaching Out*. Garden City, New York: Doubleday & Co., Inc., 1975.

Nouwen, Henri, J.M. *The Wounded Healer*. 1972; rpt. Garden City, New York: Image Books, 1979.

Ostrander, Sheila and Lynn Schroeder. *Psychic Discoveries Behing the Iron Curtain*. 1970; rpt. Englewood Cliffs, New Jersey: Bantam, 1971.

Peck, M. Scott. *The Road Less Traveled*. New York: Simon and Schuster, 1978.

Phipps, William E. *Recovering Biblical Sensuousness*. Philadelphia: Westminster, 1975.

Reusch, Bernard. Homo Spaiens: *from man to demigod*. New York: Columbia University Press, 1972.

Rose, Louis. *Faith Healing*. 1968; rpt. New York: Penguin Books, 1971.

St. Teresa of Avila. *The Interior Castle*. Introduction, XI.

St. Teresa of Avila. *The Life of St. Teresa of Avila*. Trans. E. Allison Peers. London: Sheed and Ward, 1979.

Sanborn, Hugh W. *Mental-Spiritual Health Models: An Analysis of the Models of Boisen, Hiltner and Clinebell.* Washington: University Press of America, 1979.**

Sanford, Agnes. *The Healing Light.* Rev. Ed. St. Paul, MN: Macalester Park, 1972.

Sanford, John A. *Healing and Wholeness.* New York: Paulist Press, 1977.

Siegel, Bernie S., *Love, Medicine & Healing.* New York: Harper & Row, 1986.**

Simson, Eve. *The Faith Healer.* New York: Pyramid Publications (Harcourt Brace Jovanovich, Inc.), 1977.

Swift, Edgar J. *Jungle of the Mind.* Facsimile edition (Essay Index Reprint. Series Reproduction of 1931 ed.).

Tillich, Paul. *Christianity and Encounter of the World Religions.* New York: Columbia, 1963.

Tournier, Paul. *The Healing of Persons,* Trans. Edwin Hudson. New York: Harper and Row, 1965.**

Weatherhead, Leslie. *Psychology, Religion, and Health.* London: Hodder and Stoughton, 1952.

Weil, Simone. *Waiting For God.* New York: Harper & Row, 1951.**

Woods, Richard P. "The Possession Problem," in *Begone, Satan!.* Huntington, IN: Our Sunday Visitor, Inc., 1974.

Worrall, Ambrose, with Olga N. Worrall. *The Gift of Healing.* New York: Harper and Row, 1965.**

Glossary

Apocalyptic: An adjective derived from the Greek noun *apocalypsis,* which means "revelation." It is principally used to describe a literary type (books or writings like the Book of Revelation) or a type of theology (theology like that in the Book of Revelation). "Apocalyptic Judaism," therefore, is a type of Judaism that expresses itself like the forms and theology of the Book of Revelation.

Apostasy: Going from a believing to an unbelieving stance, going to disloyalty from a former loyalty. Our word comes from a Greek word meaning to desert, abandon, or revolt from.

Before the Common Era (B.C.E.): See Common Era.

Common Era (C.E.): A more inclusive way of dating historical events than the older, more provincial way in use among Christians since the seventh century—B.C. for Before Christ and A.D. for *Anno Domini* (the year of Our Lord). Christians today are becoming more aware of the feelings and convictions of Jews and others who do not place Jesus Christ at the focal point in history. Using C.E. (Common Era) and B.C.E. (Before the Common Era) demonstrates this respect without in any sense diminishing a Christian's loyalty to Christian theology.

Etymology: The study of word origins and the history of changes and developments in the meanings of words.

Hellenistic Jews: Those Jews who adopted the language of the Hellenes (Greeks), and, in varying degrees, their cultural ways also. All the writers of the New Testament were Hellenistic Jews, except (probably) the author of the Book of Revelation. The emergence of the term "Christians" as the special name for those Jews who believed in Jesus Christ is noted in Acts 11:26. Elsewhere in the New Testament, even in Luke-Acts, what we now call "Christians" are called "believing Jews."

Incubation: The practice, common in antiquity, of seeking healing from a supernatural source by sleeping overnight in the sacred precincts of the particular supernatural power. In Egypt, temples of Imhotep (the Egyptian god of healing) were incubation centers. Among the Greeks, Asklepian shrines functioned similarly. The practice carried over into some areas of Christianity.

Irenaeus: Bishop of Lyons in Gaul (France) during the last quarter of the second century C.E. He is generally regarded as the first great Catholic theologian.

Jewish-Gnosticism: Gnosticism viewed the universe as a prison and the material world as the source of all evil. Humans were sparks of God imprisoned in a physical body. Both God and human inner selves were purely spiritual and alien to this universe. Salvation involved knowing this true God, knowing oneself to be part of God, and therefore being rescued from this prison-world. This saving knowledge (*gnosis*) was imparted by a redeemer figure who was "not of this world." Jewish Gnosticism modified this by accomodating (with difficulty) the concept of God as Creator, but in none of our sources is this accommodation satisfactorily explained.

Luke-Acts: the term coined in modern scholarship to describe the untitled 2-volume work now separated in the New Testament under individual titles, the Gospel of Luke (volume I) and the Acts of the Apostles (Volume II). The overall unity of the two volumes is easily established. Neither volume can be fully understood without the other.

Shalom: the Hebrew word of customary greeting, meaning healthy, sane, whole, complete, peaceful, safe. In Arabic, "salaam." In Germanic languages it has no exact equivalent, but parallels the German "heil" and the Anglo-Saxon "hal" or "hale." The common English translation "peace" is much too restricted to convey the full meaning of *shalom*.

Soteria: The Greek word usually translated "salvation." It means much more than salvation in the usual religious sense. It includes salvation from poor health and from all kinds of dangers and threats. It is a rescue word and includes very positive meanings of being rescued *for* something as well as *from* something. No English word translates all its meanings.

Theophilos: The addressee of the two-volume work Luke-Acts, as indicated in Luke 1:3 and Acts 1:1. Because of the honorific title in Luke 1:3, the Greek word is probably the name of an otherwise unknown official in the government of the Roman Empire. A minority opinion sees the word as referring to anyone who loves God, since the word itself is a Greek word meaning "lover of God," or "friend of God."

Weltanschauung: a German word expressing one's understanding of how human existence fits into the universe at large. "World-view" is a literal, but incomplete, way to translate it. Since English has no adequate equivalent word, it is commonly left in its German form when precision of thought requires what it says. The French "milieu" is closer than the English "environment."

136